MAKE IT BIG!

MAKE IT BIG!

HOW TO MAKE MONEY FROM YOUR MILLION-DOLLAR IDEA

*15 successful inventors
share their secrets, plus
top websites for inventors*

ALICIA BEVERLEY

ALLEN & UNWIN

First published in 2000
Allen & Unwin
9 Atchison Street, St Leonards NSW 1590 Australia
Phone: (61 2) 8425 0100
Fax: (61 2) 9906 2218
E-mail: frontdesk@allen-unwin.com.au
Web: http://www.allen-unwin.com.au

National Library of Australia
Cataloguing-in-Publication entry:

Beverly, Alicia.
    Make it big!: how to make money from your million-dollar idea.

    Includes index.
    ISBN 1 86508 191 4.

    1. Product management. 2. Inventions. 3. Inventions—Marketing.
    4. Success. I. Title.

658.5

Set in 12/14 pt Adobe Garamond by DOCUPRO, Sydney
Printed by Griffin Press Pty Ltd, South Australia

Foreword

I have been closely associated with inventors since 1970, when I commenced production of the ABC television series 'The Inventors'. When I was asked to write a foreword to *Make it Big!* I started to think, just what is an inventor? What makes them different? Why do they devote a great part of their lives to their ideas? Well, they are certainly persistent. They are optimistic—they have to be. And their original approach to bettering things is sometimes almost mystical. They can be unreasonable. Reasonable people would adapt themselves to the world instead of trying to adapt the world to themselves.

It isn't easy to get a new product accepted. It is not just a matter of coming up with a new idea that will improve our lives. If you are an inventor you need to have the good fortune to find the right path and the right help. Alicia Beverley has managed to gather into one book more good advice than most inventors are given in a life time. And advice is what inventors need. Don't be afraid to seek assistance. Remember, it might be the last key in the bunch that opens the door to success.

Having a good idea does not mean that people will realise its potential. The great Leonardo da Vinci, who conceived so many incredible machines, rarely found an outlet for them. In fact, it is possible that none of them were ever commercialised. Once you have a good idea the real work commences, from protecting your intellectual property, to making a prototype, deciding how you want to handle the manufacturing and distribution and, finally, getting the public to accept something new. If you are an expert in all these fields you won't need *Make it Big!*, but I believe that very few people can bridge the gap from inspiration to commercial acceptance without a lot of expert advice.

My work keeps me in touch with inventors in Australia and overseas. So many of them would like a magic wand to wave, bringing them recognition and fortune. There is no magic wand. The development of any idea takes time, effort and money. Thomas Alva Edison, the great American inventor, reported that he made very little profit from actually inventing. His success mostly came as a manufacturer through the introduction and sale of his inventions. But don't be discouraged. Remember that when Edison's electric light was submitted to the British Post Office in the 1870s the chief engineer, Sir William Preece, dogmatically declared that it was an idiotic idea.

I believe that *Make it Big!* will become the handbook for anyone who is moving into the world of innovations and inventions. Take the hand that is offered. Don't try to do everything yourself. Learn from the mistakes of others, because you can't live long enough to make them all yourself.

New ideas should be fostered like children. One of my favourite stories concerns the great American statesman Benjamin Franklin who, in 1783, was watching the first flight of the montgolfier hot-air balloon over Paris. One of the bystanders asked, 'What use is it?'. Franklin replied, 'What use is a new-born baby!'. And that is what inventions are—new-born babies. Once they are conceived they must be realised, loved, developed and seen to their full potential.

My wish to all inventors is that one day their name should figure in the dictionary of proper nouns. It is possibly the crowning of an inventor's career that his or her name should become a common proper noun. Rudolf Diesel, Louis Braille, Samuel Plimsoll, King Camp Gillette, John Kellogg and Lazio Biro are just some of the people who have left their name stamped on their inventions. So let this be your goal—to one day have your name in the dictionary, describing your invention.

BEVERLEY GLEDHILL, OAM
AUSTRALIAN DELEGATE
INTERNATIONAL EXHIBITION OF INVENTIONS
GENEVA

Dedicated to Michael, my parents and Marje

Contents

The Expert Panel

I have pulled together my own 'expert panel' from the many quiet achievers around Australia who use their experience and expertise to help inventors turn their great ideas into a money-making success.

This panel also includes the inventors who have added their stories to mine so that you might benefit from their commercialisation experiences: Michael Beverley, Shane Cavanaugh, Graham Due, Peter Eaton, Willie Erken, Sue Ismiel, John McNamee, Max Moorhouse, John Sinclair, Joan Stuckey, Peter Thorne, Robert Webster, Paul Willett and Warren Wilson.

I am grateful to them all for their time, enthusiasm, insight and input.

Zeke Ezra, Senior Partner, Duesburys Chartered Accountants

Zeke Ezra is a senior partner with one of Australia's largest chartered accountancy firms, Duesburys. Along with his expertise with accountancy, taxation and investment issues, he has helped raise millions of dollars for Australian innovators.

Peter Fisher, Patent Attorney, Senior Partner, Fisher Adams and Kelly

Peter Fisher is a senior partner of one of Australia's leading patent and trade mark attorney firms, Fisher Adams and Kelly. His experience has helped hundreds of inventors with their intellectual property protection requirements.

He is also the chairman of PacRim Technomart, an international showcase for Australian and overseas innovators to market their products and research capabilities.

Beverley Gledhill, OAM, Official Ambassador to the Geneva International Exhibition of Inventions, and Director of Gledhill Belfanti Productions

Beverley Gledhill was awarded an Order of Australia Medal for services to Australian inventors. She tirelessly promotes Aussie inventors and their inventions on radio, TV and in the press. Since 1975, she has been the official Australian delegate to the prestigious International Exhibition of Inventions and New Techniques, held annually in Geneva, Switzerland.

Together with her partner, Paul Belfanti, producer and director of such programs as 'The Inventors' and 'What'll They Think of Next', she runs Gledhill Belfanti Productions, specialising in video production, media exposure, public relations and representation at the Geneva International Exhibition of Inventions.

Andrew Holt, Director, A.R. Holt & Associates and former President of the Canberra Inventors' Association

Andrew Holt has dedicated himself to helping Australian inventors, and has personally assisted numerous inventors over the past few years in every area of inventing and commercialising. He has extensive experience with advanced levels of product commercialisation, including breakthrough approaches to finance.

Gary McCay, past National and Queensland President, Inventors' Association of Australia

Gary McCay has an engineering and business management background. He is a seasoned inventor and has experienced all the highs and lows of product commercialisation. In his role as Federal and Queensland President of the Inventors' Association of Australia, he helped other inventors get on the right track to successfully launching their product idea.

John Levey, Prototyper, Owner, John Levey & Associates

John Levey is an industrial designer and prototyper with 15 years' experience. He has worked closely with many inventors and is aware of the unique needs they have when transforming their great ideas into a tangible form.

Disclaimer

The inclusion of these individuals does not constitute a referral to them or their organisations.

Acknowledgements

I would like to thank Gary Kichenside, Director of Intellectual Property Promotions at IP Australia, and his terrific team. When Gary came to IP Australia, the government organisation that incorporates the Patents, Trade Marks and Designs Offices, it was then known as the Australian Industrial Property Organisation (AIPO), and the information available for inventors was inadequate and often downright confusing. In fact, many of the inventors featured in this book mentioned that the lack of useful materials from AIPO actually hindered their commercialisation efforts, and there was no other resource for inventing guidance.

I was commissioned as a freelance writer to work with Gary and his team to create dynamic and helpful information kits and other materials, jargon-free articles and case studies of how real inventors and innovative business people had used patents, and registered trademarks and designs, to their advantage. The products and services the IP promotions team created, most of which are free, are now enormously helpful and some are unique in the world. I thank IP Australia for allowing the inclusion of some of the case studies written during my work with Gary and his team.

I would also like to thank Chris Kaine, owner of Business Angels Pty Ltd, Dr Robyn Lindley, manager of the Illawarra Innovation Centre, and Warren Hough, also of the Illawarra Innovation Centre, Barry Masters, owner of Barry Masters and Associates, Brandon Keene of the Australian Design Awards, Philip Mendes, technology transfer lawyer, and Anne Buchner, series producer of Channel Nine's 'Small Business Show'.

Introduction

This is the book that I wish I had had when I began inventing in the early 1990s. Like most inventors I had a great idea, but didn't know what to do next. Amazingly, I did manage to get my first product idea commercialised. It made it onto the shop shelves in Australia and in the tough American market. By this time, however, I had made every mistake in the book. Although most inventors are naturally creative, optimistic, self-starters, independent, persistent and hard workers, they tend to fall victim to the same mistakes.

But this book is about making money from *your* great idea, not about making mistakes. It is a step-by-step guide to getting your great idea from your mind onto the shop shelves. You will need to gain skills and knowledge you may not have had before. But just imagine the potential rewards!

MY OWN STORY AS AN INVENTOR

How long would you wait to see whether your product became a success? Two years, four years, five years? How about six?

On the face of it, my three-in-one baby product had all the hallmarks of immediate success. And unlike many inventors I had the benefit of my professional marketing, writing and public relations skills, giving me the ability to easily promote my product and myself. From very early on, success appeared to be a sure thing. It had to be, because I took enormous risks by filing for a provisional patent application and accruing patent attorney and official fees I couldn't afford. I then made matters worse financially by leaving my part-time position to aggressively seek a licensee for my product idea.

I began commercialisation by researching potential manufacturers/distributors through looking at similar products available at department stores. I targeted a handful, made contact, and then travelled to Melbourne for a day of meetings. My first meeting was quite simply humiliating. I was dismissed as just another of the 'crazy mums who think they have the next best thing to sliced bread', and was practically booted out of the office. I considered heading straight for the airport, but instead gritted my teeth and headed out to the next meeting.

I went from humiliation to exhilaration when My Place®, 'the handy bag that's a playmat and sleepingbag too', was readily licensed by a well-established Australian manufacturer/ distributor of similar nappy bag-type products. Then the problems began, and they simply never stopped.

The bags were manufactured in China. A perfect sample would arrive for approval. Then an entire shipment would arrive that bore no resemblance to the approved sample. Quality control problems included snaps that would chip or even fly off—alarming problems for any product, but terrifying for a baby product. These setbacks began to wear on the manufacturer, and in the end we parted company with very little to show for many months of hard work.

The irony was that my public relations and marketing efforts always paid off beautifully. I was interviewed in the press and on radio and TV. The popular *Australia's Parents*

Magazine continually gave My Place® top billing in its product reviews. My efforts led to letters and phone calls from women all around the country wanting to buy a product for which I had no stock.

Though I was terribly demoralised by this, I had my parents in America conduct similar research on potential licensees. I contacted one of their suggested targets, a large and well-known bag manufacturer. To my amazement, they were immediately enthusiastic, and it looked as if I had hit 'the big time' again.

I then won the Canberra region Inventor of the Year and the product won Invention of the Year. I was on a high. Then the familiar production problems reared their ugly head. I felt cursed. It took a long time to solve these problems. Eventually I felt confident enough to order stock for Australia, but was stunned when box after box contained defective goods. I was stuck with a huge freight bill and hundreds of bags littering my garage that I would never be able to sell. I was saddled with an overdraft and loan to cover patent and other intellectual property expenses, and I simply could not service the payments. It was a disaster.

The term of the licence agreement ended and I began to look for other licensees. Over a year or more, the bag was rejected by roughly a dozen Australian and American companies. I had lost thousands of dollars. In the end I literally put the bag in a box and shelved the whole idea. Or so I thought. I was constantly niggled by the feeling that the product deserved a go. Yet I didn't feel the answer lay in finding another licensee.

That's when it hit me. Why not sell *the idea*, not the product? My gut instinct told me that there are a lot of women who need extra cash to make ends meet. They are looking for a cottage industry-level enterprise that does not take a lot of cash to start up. They do not want to be small business people because of the commitment needed and the connotations that has in this country, but they would consider a 'mini business'.

I advertised My Place® as a money-making opportunity in a national craft magazine and was amazed by the response. The phone rang off the hook and the orders for my $195 mini business kit flooded in, which included a professional pattern, woven labels, swing tags, marketing tools, and marketing and sewing guides. I was selling opportunity, not a product. It took six years to arrive at this point, but in a few short weeks I made more money out of My Place® than I had with two major licensees.

When I look back at the first few years to determine where I 'went wrong', I am unable to come to any conclusions. Certainly I was naive and made every classic mistake. There was also a measure of sheer bad luck. At the same time, getting a product on the market at all, especially on the tough American market, is an accomplishment I am proud of. I have now found the *right* way to market this product and it uses my strongest skills—writing and organisation. I am able to avoid the hassles of self-manufacturing and the agony of licensing. Not to mention that the profit margin for information products beats that for manufacturing and licensing hands down.

Your product idea could bring you regular royalty payments, as it has for Warren Wilson, the inventor of Better Blocks™, a deceptively simple design that has sold over 600 million units around the world. Or your great idea could be the basis of a successful business, as Sue Ismiel, creator of Nad's® hair-removal gel, has found. Starting from her own kitchen, Sue created a dynamic manufacturing enterprise with millions of dollars in turnover, producing and selling tens of thousands of units annually. Both Warren and Sue, as well as all of the other inventors featured in this book, told me they had desperately needed commercialisation guidance when they first started out.

When I told the inventors about the information this book would contain, many of them sighed and said, 'Wow, I wish I'd had that book!'.

And now *you* have it. If you are ready to transform your great idea into a money-maker, this is the book for you. I am positive that if you read and follow this book's suggestions, your idea will be more refined, more commercially viable, and more likely to succeed. You will also have the knowledge you need to avoid the classic pitfalls that slow inventors down or actually stop them in their tracks. This book will show you how to make smart choices with your time and money, so that you can commercialise your great idea as soon as possible.

Congratulations on your great idea. Now let's get started.

ALICIA BEVERLEY
AUGUST 1999

1 Be a Successful Inventor

This book features 15 successful Australian inventors, including myself. Real people, many with jobs and regular lives, who had a flash of brilliance and managed to transform their raw concept into an actual product. Most had never commercialised a new product before, or even known anyone who had.

After years as a squash coach and of running his own courts, Max Moorhouse was convinced he could find a way to protect players from high-speed squash balls. His solution, i-Max®, has now been endorsed world wide, and under-19 players are required to wear i-Max® eyewear during some competitions.

PROFESSIONAL COACHING EXPERIENCE LEADS TO VITAL INVENTION

If you play squash or have watched a match you will know that the squash ball slams from racket to wall and back again at bullet-like speeds. The potential for eye injury is a reality even for top competitors, but especially for younger or novice players.

As a professional coach and former owner of a popular squash facility in Gosford, New South Wales, Max Moorhouse had faced this reality for years. By giving his young players the best skills possible, he aimed to counteract the dangers associated with the game—and to allay parents' fears. But, as Max points out, accidents do happen, and the eye is the last place you want to cop a ball flying at 100 or more km/hour. 'Strangely enough, though the risks are evident to anyone, our sport as an industry is only now coming to grips with this injury factor', says Moorhouse.

Moorhouse tackled the protective eyewear issue for years, at times attempting to design his own solution but always on the lookout for an existing product that would fit the bill. The eyewear needed to be tough enough to withstand a direct hit without shattering or breaking, give the player totally unobstructed peripheral vision from any position, so flexible that it didn't feel foreign to the player, and of a design calibre that would make it attractive to the industry at large. Time and time again Moorhouse came up empty-handed.

Finally, he approached a friend who was also a designer. 'I had him draw up what I felt was the absolute "ants pants"', says Moorhouse. But when he went around to injection moulders with the design, he was given quotes of around $40 000 just for the mould, and everything came to a halt. He and his wife headed to Tasmania for a holiday and were so smitten that they decided to settle in the Huon Valley. They sold up in Gosford—the house, the squash club, the lot.

Moorhouse took up coaching once again, and began in earnest to crack the protective eyewear problem. He eventually created an eyewear design that eliminates the need for costly moulds. It features a crystal-clear shield that wraps from temple to temple and is held in place by a cushioned forehead band connected to an adjustable strap.

Though Moorhouse had lived with the potential of his concept for so long, like most inventors he had no idea how to bring his concept from an idea to a commercial reality:

> I was completely green, and I found that I lurched from one pitfall to another due to a sheer lack of information about what the commercialisation process involves and how the patent system works. I really needed someone to sit down with me and spell it all out, because I needed direction.

In January 1994 he lodged his own provisional patent application with the Patents Office of IP Australia (then the Australian Industrial Property Organisation). The provisional application gave Moorhouse 12 months to refine his product even further and move into prototype development before making the decision to file a 'complete' application.

In hindsight, Moorhouse wishes that he had consulted a patent attorney to lodge this first application as well as for some insight into the new realm of patent fees he had just bought into:

> I soon realised that having a patent and trying to support the costs of maintaining that patent is another issue entirely. If you aren't careful, your costs can send you broke, so it's important that patenting is aligned with commercial activity and viability. If you can't sell it, you can't make your patent payments. And perhaps you shouldn't have a patent in the first place.

By December of that year Moorhouse had hired patent attorneys and filed another provisional application based on significant improvements resulting from his prototype: 'I went for broke and also filed a design registration for the look of the eyewear and a registered trademark for the "i-Max" name at the same time.' Also in December, Moorhouse offered a partnership to a close friend, a retired business executive and squash coach in his 40s who speaks several languages, has expertise in finance, marketing and information technology, and tremendous overseas networks. It was at this point that things really took off:

> The injection of finance was important, but being able to share the vision with someone of my partner's calibre was just as significant for me as it was for the product.

Now, protected to the hilt, it was time to trial i-Max™ openly with competition-level players and get the kind of gritty assessment essential to the product's development. An initial product run was ordered with Laughlin Manufacturing in Margate, and sponsorship contracts with players from the Kingborough Squash Club in Kingston were arranged.

Innovative in itself, the contract stipulated that every time the player picked up a racket he or she must wear the i-Max™ eyewear and branded T-shirt and at the end of the trial provide comprehensive feedback. 'We listened to what players had to say and it did result in the product being somewhat modified', says Moorhouse. 'We then moved immediately into local marketing.' What happened next was a gratifying confirmation of Moorhouse's vision: 'There was wide acceptance of the product. We had applications from other squash clubs for stocks of the eyewear.'

At this point, market share in Australia alone is enormous. In this country it is compulsory for all players under 19 and their coaches to wear protective eyewear. Of this group, Moorhouse estimates that 90% choose i-Max™. Since 1 January 1999, the European Squash Federation has also required all players under 19 years of age to wear protective eyewear; i-Max™ eyewear is the preferred product, and has now been endorsed by international teams and the World, European, Asian and Australian Squash Federations. The accolades and achievements keep rolling in.

i-Max™ eyewear is protected internationally through intellectual property rights and is now distributed to 22 countries. The product has also been certified for the Australian/New Zealand and US safety standards for racquet sports protective eyewear. The eyewear is safe for a direct hit to the eyes and upper face from a ball travelling at 150 km/hour.

Though the product is clearly a success, Moorhouse is realistic:

> We are talking about protective eyewear, not a mass product that every household has a need for. But the business supports itself and we have recouped our R&D [research and development] expenses. Of course, our intellectual property protection expenses—the patent, the design registration and the registered trademark—are ongoing.

Max Moorhouse's determination to find a way to prevent potentially disabling injuries for squash players has paid off—not only for him personally but for everyone who loves the sport. He also has valuable advice for anyone starting out 'green', as he was when he embarked on the road to commercialisation:

> Find out as much as you can before you commit yourself. Talk to patent attorneys, ring your state office of IP Australia—they have a lot of helpful free information now, which was not available when I started out. No idea is worth losing your home over; and having a great idea is not a guarantee to success. But starting out with an understanding of the complex nature of commercialisation is at least the first step.

Peter Thorne, a retired engineer living in a rural area where grass can get out of control in spring, struggled with inadequate brushcutters. He felt existing cutters simply could not make the grade, so he went into his workshop and designed Weedwakka®, a hardy, practical favourite at agricultural shows around the country.

Shane Cavanaugh was a theatre scrub nurse with a young family. His invention, BladeSafe®, is an ergonomic, dynamically designed receptacle for sharp instruments used in surgery. It replaces the kidney dish, which is incorrectly used for this purpose in hospitals everywhere. The product has the potential to change the handling protocol for 'sharps' around the world.

What these inventors share is a tremendous faith in their concept and, importantly, faith in themselves. Once they had had their 'Eureka!' moment, where the proverbial lightbulb flashed on and their great idea was born, these inventors found that the real work had only just begun. Unfortunately, almost all of them lacked the kind of specific direction that inventors need, and most fell victim to the pitfalls associated with commercialising new products. But in the end, and against enormous odds, each of them was successful.

From my own experience as an inventor, and from talking to inventors and people who assist new product hopefuls, I have put together a list of positive attributes shared by successful inventors. I recommend that you take their hard-earned insight to heart, as well as doing your best to avoid the mistakes that inventors tend to make, also included in this chapter.

Top 5 attributes of successful inventors

Persevere. Stick with your idea even when times are bleak, so long as you are being true to your personal goals, the budget is not being blown out and there is still a strong chance for success. It took several years before Max Moorhouse realised his dream of sporting eyewear that met his stringent parameters for safety, appropriateness and player comfort. It also took me a few years before I found the best way to market my own product. Though there was a time when I actually shelved my first product, I always believed it was special and destined for success, and my belief in it and myself has now been repaid.

Pace yourself and your money. If you use your resources wisely, you will not find yourself suddenly in debt and burned out. Peter Thorne decided not to pursue the mass manufacturing of his product, Weedwakka®: instead, he makes and sells each unit, building slowly as the product gains acceptance within the tough agricultural market. Sue Ismiel says: 'Take risks, but only ones you can support with your current resources. And avoid debt.'

Conduct comprehensive research and development. Give your product the time it needs to evolve. Michael Beverley spent two and a half years developing his innovative Living Picture® process. His commitment to gruelling R&D has paid off. The process is now licensed by a major giftware manufacturer for the production of exclusive coffee mugs that feature famous licensed imagery. Robert Webster, Gold Coast surfer and business owner, laughs when he remembers how he and his employee conducted R&D by trialling his new surfer eyewear concept 'on the back beaches' to keep it under wraps: 'There were a lot of early mornings at isolated beaches to make sure the eyewear would do what I wanted it to do.'

Network, and create a circle of advisers. Never work in isolation. Use advisers whenever you can. Don't hesitate to make contacts and ask questions. Shane Cavanaugh knew he didn't know enough about the commercialisation process to ensure success for BladeSafe®. He sought the help of his local inventors' association, and made an important contact that helped introduce him to an entire network of experts. He took networking one step further, as many of the people he spoke to have now become investors. I sought help from as many quarters as possible. I regularly speak to my accountant, seek advice from a close contact in the inventing arena, have spoken to a variety of business advisers and generally seek out contacts in areas of commercialisation that I need assistance with. I also create new networks with people in areas of different industries from which I need to gain knowledge, for instance by making contacts in the plastics industry.

Believe in yourself and your product, but don't be afraid to walk away. You have to find a fine balance between having a deep faith in yourself and your product idea and at the same time not being so emotionally attached that you cannot walk away when the signs are not good. Paul Willett has a 15-point 'torture test' that all prospective products must survive. Says Paul, 'This way we don't spend our valuable money and energy attempting to commercialise something that can't make the grade. Yes, all of my ideas are my babies, but they can also be expensive mistakes.' If a product concept does makes it past this preparatory period, R&D for each product is significant and has cost many thousands of dollars. This level of expense is certainly justified, as Paul's products are groundbreaking and have shaped the current baking industry.

Willie Erken feels that salesmanship was important to his success. Willie was a professional window cleaner for many years, but when he became unemployed and took part in a self-employment scheme he designed an innovative, ergonomic window-cleaning tool. Willie is an upbeat, positive person who always has a smile on his face. His enthusiasm is infectious, and this has probably been instrumental in his success. However, if this doesn't come naturally to you, don't despair. Two of the most successful inventors profiled in this book, Warren Wilson and Paul

Willett, felt that they were consistently unable to portray their inventions' potential.

LOVING THE JOB EVERYONE HATES

The first thing you notice about Willie Erken's home office is that the windows are exceptionally clean. In fact, it's safe to say they aren't just clean—they are actually crystal clear. But this is what you would expect from the man behind the most innovative window-cleaning implements in Australia, possibly the world.

Willie Erken's 15 years as a top window cleaner, with his own crew and small business, gave him a shrewd insight into the job everyone hates. What set Willie on the road to an award-winning product, though, was an obsession with perfecting window cleaning into one action, where each stroke both cleaned and dried a window. Ironically, it was after selling his window-cleaning business and a failed venture into importing Indonesian goods that Willie found himself in a position to pursue his goal to create the perfect window-cleaning tool. Unemployed, Willie decided to take part in the New Enterprise Incentive Scheme (NEIS) program, where participants form teams centred on a new product or service idea, and develop a workable business plan.

Willie's team chose his prototype pivoting window cleaner. Halfway through the business plan process, he experienced the proverbial Eureka!:

> Suddenly I saw that the current prototype was limited by having only an up and down pivoting action. This helped to switch from the cleaning strip to the drying pad, but the product was still awkward to use. The answer was to add a lateral pivot so that the cleaning head swung easily in an arcing motion with only a small flick of the wrist.

The next day Willie had his patent attorney make a 'provisional' patent application with the Patent Office of

IP Australia. For around a $1200 investment, this gave Willie 12 months' breathing space before he needed to commit to a 'complete' application and further fees. It also gave him a set of pre-patent benefits, which are cemented when a patent is formally granted, sometimes years later. The day Willie's application was accepted by IP Australia—the 'priority date'—established a formal point from which he could claim ownership of the invention. It also enabled him to pursue commercialisation activities knowing that he had begun the patent process, a measure of protection in itself.

Willie's team went on to win the 1991 Business Plan Award for New South Wales. But it was a chance meeting with an old friend, Peter St Vincent Welch, an ex-CSIRO scientist with significant experience in commercialising break-throughs, that initiated real progress. They became business partners and successfully applied for an AusIndustry research and development grant to enable them to develop prototype tooling. One of the provisos of this grant was the commission-ing of an ergonomic report. Conducted by the University of NSW, the report found that the window-cleaning tool was exceptionally easy to use and took stress off the user's wrist. It was showcased as a model product at an ergonomic con-ference. 'Because it is objective and so favourable, the report has really become a selling point', says Willie. 'What's exciting is that we can see so many applications for this approach in the entire cleaning tool industry, not just window cleaners.'

Now on a roll, the two partners snaffled an AusIndustry concessional loan with great terms—first three years interest free, with interest paid at a percentage of commercial rates for the last three years. They then attended the Interclean Convention in Amsterdam to gain product feedback, but were inundated with enquiries. One enthusiastic manufac-turer gave his version of product endorsement by presenting the two with a 24 carat gold miniature squeegee. 'Everyone wanted to do a deal. We were really pleased with what we heard, and it did lead to some important improvements', says St Vincent Welch.

Not only does the team hold patent protection in a number of countries, they have also registered their distinctive trademark, Wagtail®, which fits the product's main feature perfectly:

> We were in the middle of a major brainstorming session for a really great name when my wife just came out with, 'Wagtail. You know, like Willie Wagtail. The fan on the bird's tail'. We just looked at her and knew that was the one.

The trademark and the ® symbol denoting it as registered are used on the product itself, in advertisements, on business cards and so on. The TM symbol is also used on the phrase they use consistently with their logo, 'The pivotal change in cleaning'.

There is now a range of Wagtail® products retailing around Australia, primarily in professional cleaning outlets, but these are expected to move into mainstream stores soon. A product that incorporates a floor-cleaning application is under negotiation with the American Home Shopping Network. Orders are now being received from around the world.

The awards are also coming thick and fast. In 1996 Wagtail® took out the Best Innovation of Australia Award at the Perth Home Show. It has gone on to win a gold medal for the Wagtail® Combi™ at the prestigious Geneva Exhibition of Inventions. As well, Willie was asked to take part in a six-month display of innovative Australian products at the Powerhouse Museum in Sydney. Says Willie:

> We believe in our own products. That's why we have devoted years and more money than I care to think about, but to see other people realise their worth . . . That's just terrific.

Sounds like payback time for the man who loves the job everyone hates.

Gary McCay, past Federal and Queensland President of the Inventors' Association of Australia, believes that a supportive home environment is important to successfully commercialising new products. This is very true, but in my view it works both ways. While you need to have your partner's and your family's unqualified support, you also need to ensure that you do not expose them to unnecessary financial risk. There is nothing like being unable to pay for normal household expenses, because you have just commissioned expensive market research, to create family tension.

Top 10 attributes of successful inventions

Why do some inventions make it and others not? That might seem like a difficult question, but there is a logical answer. Along with how capable the inventors are and their approach to commercialisation, successful inventions do have many attributes in common. Take your idea through the following list, checking how many of these points apply.

1. *Unique and novel, or a significant improvement on an existing product.* Each of the products featured in this book is completely unique or is somehow an improvement on an existing product. There are some products that do both, in the sense that they are a complete departure from what has come before, and are therefore a great improvement on what is currently available. One example is John McNamee's product, which looks and acts completely differently from every other life-saving device currently on the market. In fact, it is so novel that it pushes the boundaries of the official standards authority, Standards Australia.

2. *Instantly recognisable features.* In general, most products have only seconds to attract the consumer. My own handy bag is three products in one. That alone is

enough to stop some consumers in their tracks: instantly they recognise that this product has something different to offer.

3. *Inexpensive to produce or manufacture.* Cost should be no more than 20% of the retail price—less, if at all possible—to be competitive. Warren Wilson's blocks are made for around 1 cent each, and sell for several hundred per cent more at retail. One of the features of Michael Beverley's mug-decoration process is that it lessens manufacturing cost and effort considerably, compared with traditional processes.

4. *Can be manufactured with existing machinery and/or known processes.* This is one of Paul Willett's 'torture test' points for assessing new product concepts. There are many famous inventions that have also required the development of new manufacturing techniques or new technology, but these inventions are extremely expensive to take through R&D and to commercialise.

ROBOTIC MIXER REVOLUTIONISES THE BAKING INDUSTRY

Paul Willett has been described by his patent attorney as a truly amazing inventor. When faced with a problem, Willett, an engineer, instantly 'sees' the solution. The invention is so complete in his mind, he can bypass the drafting stage and simply produce the complete prototype.

His reputation has brought him many a tough challenge, but perhaps none more difficult than the one brought to him by a company looking for a solution to a labour-intensive aspect of the baking industry. Says Willett:

When enormous amounts of dough are being mixed, the issue of dividing it into equal, de-gassed portions, forming it into loaves and sending these on to baking, normally requires a lot of handling and is very time-consuming. What I have developed is a robotic head that sits inside the mixing bowl and performs every task except loaf making. Then the de-gassed portion moves on to another machine I designed, which creates loaves or rolls.

These two inventions, though they sound remarkably simple, have literally revolutionised the 'make up plant', key machinery in the baking industry worth a billion dollars in worldwide sales yearly.

Willett's machines will bring his business over $200 million in turnover over the life of their patents. They are used by some of the biggest household names in Australia and around the world. Yet for Willett inventing is as much about knowing what to drop as it is about pursuing a winner:

We have a 15-point 'torture list' which each and every idea must be able to proceed through successfully or it never sees the light of day. This way we don't spend our valuable money and energy commercialising something that can't make the grade.

The following are a few of these points. A new idea must:

- have real advantages over existing designs;
- be able to be made with existing machinery and use component parts right off the shelf where possible;
- be able to conform to all standards;
- be able to be built and sold at a profit;
- be patentable, and not able to be copied with simple changes;
- have design appeal;
- be compact, and not take up too much area;
- be serviceable and have a long life;
- be easily cleaned to maintain hygiene standards.

Following this strict regimen isn't always easy, says Willett: 'I'm just like every other inventor. My ideas are my babies. But I am running a business and I am in this game to make money.' Along with making money, Willett says you must also be willing to spend money on the necessities of inventing.

The licence agreement alone for the two bakehouse machines cost $65 000. Willett also has hefty commercial solicitor bills for the other legal contracts, such as confidentiality and employee agreements. R&D cost $1.6 million. Patent, design and trademark registration costs are in the tens of thousands.

By all standards, Willett is a successful inventor. Yet he finds his vision for an invention almost impossible to get across, even to his father. As a result, he has avoided seeking investment for this, his most important invention:

> I find I cannot get people enthusiastic until after the machine is built. By that time I have spent the money, so we have had to self-fund ourselves up to the stage where a working prototype can be demonstrated.

Willett advises inventors to cultivate a close and open working relationship with their patent attorneys. 'Inventing is an expensive business. So make your patent attorney your best friend', he laughs.

5. *Inexpensive to distribute.* It should not be heavy, and should have no complex packaging requirements. My mini business kit is essentially a paper-based product, involving a paper pattern, 27 pages of marketing and sewing guides, paper swing tags and cloth labels. The kit thus moves through most overseas countries' customs authorities without duty or hassles. Many of the inventions featured in this book are light plastic products. The exceptions are products like Paul Willett's and John Sinclair's, which are not mass market products. They are big-ticket items, so this point does not apply.

6. *Not limited to one distribution type.* For instance, it could be sold via the Internet, through direct marketing, as

well as through conventional retail venues. Several of the inventions featured here have used unexpected forms of distribution to great success. Better Blocks® and Nad's®, for example, were both launched via television infomercials; orders are taken through telemarketing centres via 1800 (freecall) numbers. Weedwakka® is sold primarily through agricultural trade fairs, and could also be sold at hardware stores alongside the products it is designed to replace. Many of the products featured here, such as Flube®, could be sold via mail order, as well as through traditional retail venues.

7. *Appeals to a large audience.* If this is not possible, it should appeal to an easily identifiable, easy-to-target niche audience. Of the inventions in this book, Better Blocks® and Flube® appeal to a relatively large audience. The rest appeal to specific but easily identifiable niche markets, such as Wagtail® cleaning products, aimed at the professional cleaning market, i-Max® eyewear, designed for squash players, and GroGuard®, designed specifically for vignerons anxious to pamper baby grape vines.

8. *Benefits are easy to explain and easy to market.* Most inventions are designed as improvements to existing products and so usually have one or more striking differences. The inventor's challenge is to ensure that these special features are well articulated so that potential consumers can quickly understand why they have to have the new product.

9. *Can easily meet all regulatory requirements.* Nad's® and Universal™ power track are utterly different products, sold to different markets, yet both must meet regulatory requirements.

10. *Design is dynamic and professional.* BladeSafe® was designed by a professional, highly regarded industrial

designer at considerable expense. This has enabled the product to gain recognition from major investors, and to become a finalist in Australia's only national industrial design competition (see Appendix).

Succeed with your invention

Time, money and effort commitment

You may need to pursue your invention on a part-time basis while you hold down a job or run your business. But to make meaningful progress, you will need to commit at least 10 hours a week to your invention's progress. This commitment on your part will include:

- R&D time to determine your idea's commercial potential, and to refine your idea so that it is ready to be expressed in some tangible form, such as a prototype or rendering. You will also need time on the Internet, in libraries and at state offices of IP Australia to conduct free searches, and regular visits to places where products similar to your product idea are sold;
- local, interstate and perhaps international telephone calls and faxes; postal charges;
- time and money to get your idea into a form others can consider and evaluate, such as a prototype, full colour rendering or miniature. (You may also want to use a confidentiality agreement at this point, either written by a solicitor or gained from your inventors' club or another source.) This will all probably involve expert help at an hourly fee;
- targeting and networking with 'insiders' in the relevant industry, and with other inventors/innovators through your local inventors' club meetings for information-gathering and moral support (you will not be asked for details of your idea and do not offer any);

- time and money to meet business advisers, such as accountants and solicitors. There are also Business Enterprise Centre advisers available, generally for free advice, in most states and territories, and occasionally these BECs have arrangements with local professionals, which can involve lower fees and even free time;
- time and money to meet specialist intellectual property advisers, such as patent and trademark attorneys (first visits are usually free of charge);
- time and money to make and be in touch with contacts directly related to getting your product on the market, such as potential manufacturers and/or distributors.

How much money will I need?

I have not yet met an inventor, successful or otherwise, who spent less than $2000 of his or her own money. I have known and have heard of inventors who have spent $100 000 and more, mainly due to intellectual property protection costs and overseas commercialisation activity (see Chapter 3). I know of inventors who have put their job, house, personal savings and family loans on the line—and have lost everything, a common result of the 'inventor's syndrome'.

Most inventors can expect to lay out between $2000 (at the barest minimum) and $10 000 (more commonly) of personal funds in a time-frame spanning a few months to several years. A realistic figure would be about $5000. By this point you should have made significant progress, and have a solid idea of your product's commercial viability. Factors that can influence the amount you spend include:

- how long it takes for you to drop your idea, or to be successful;
- your own abilities and expertise in areas relating to commercialisation, as well as the networks and relation-

ships you can call on for help so that you spend the bare minimum on external assistance;

■ the amount of effort and depth you put into every stage of commercialisation, such as R&D and determining your idea's commercial viability;

■ how, and in which countries, you decide to protect your idea and whether or not you self-file your applications for protection or use the services of trademark and patent attorneys (I do not recommend self-filing your patent applications, but domestic trademarks and design registrations tend to be relatively straightforward);

■ how involved your invention or idea is;

■ whether or not you are successful in gaining investment dollars or loans, whether from family and friends or an institution such as a bank or credit union (see Chapter 4);

■ whether or not you decide to license your product to another party or self-manufacture, either at home on a small scale or through establishing full-scale manufacturing capabilities; and

■ how many and what type of service-providers you use, such as professionals, tradespeople, graphic artists, market researchers, marketing and PR people.

One word of caution: document everything you do carefully as you go along. Set up whatever filing system works for you and diligently keep it active and complete. Retain all bills, receipts, official documents, letters, faxes, press coverage and so on.

Bringing your product to market

These main stages of commercialisation are a guide only, primarily because you may revisit various steps at times and achieve others concurrently. It is important to note, though, that you will almost certainly self-fund at least the first seven to eight stages, because your idea will need at least basic protection and it is vital not to seek protection until it is in a final, well-tested form. As well, most investors, bank managers, potential partners and licensees are not willing to get involved financially until the idea is complete and well protected. They will also require a significant amount of supporting material to prove viability (see Chapter 2).

Clearly, if you choose to become a self-manufacturer (or contract a manufacturer that will provide you with your finished product), there will be a point when your commercialisation activity takes a totally different path from that of someone looking to license their idea to another party. Self-manufacturing usually means that you are also responsible for distributing and selling your product. The following are the main stages of successful commercialisation. To differentiate them from licensing activity, self-manufacturing stages combine an 'm' with the stage number.

1. Intensive research to ensure your idea is worth taking to the next step.

2. Development of your product until it is fully evolved and refined to your capability.

3. Tangible expression of your idea into a prototype, rendering, miniature etc. so that it can be considered by others (this often results in even further refinement).

4. Preparation of a comprehensive presentation package to enable you to 'sell' your idea to people who might be important to commercialisation.

5. A basic protection of your idea to enable you to begin showing it around; this stage may or may not involve assistance from patent and trademark attorneys.

6. Gaining any official approvals needed from local, state

and federal regulatory bodies, including ensuring that your product complies with mandatory standards.

7. Seeking assistance from other service-providers, such as accountants, business advisers and commercial solicitors.

8. Seeking finance or investment as needed.

9. Researching potential licensees for your idea.

9m. Researching the self-manufacturing option, including all the costs of establishing a manufacturing business— whether on a cottage-industry scale (recommended to start) or on a mass scale—such as a variety of business insurance needs, overhead costs, occupational health and safety issues.

10m. Creating a business plan.

11m. Preparing your product for retail sale by gaining a barcode number (if needed) from EAN Australia Pty Ltd, the organisation which dispenses these codes for all new products (see Appendix), and determining what sales tax applies.

12m. Trialling of the product on a small scale for as long as possible to iron out production problems and ensure that sales are possible.

13m. Full establishment of self-manufacturing.

14m. Launch and distribution of your self-manufactured product.

10. Communicating with your potential licensee and awaiting approval.

11. Negotiating with your potential licensee on actual approval of the product or from the point of expressed interest in principle (either you or a solicitor acting on your behalf).

12. Finalisation of a licensing agreement with your licensee.

13. Establishing a working relationship with your licensee, if this is included in your agreement (i.e. to refine the product for the marketplace, marketing, PR).

14. Manufacturing of the product by your licensee.

15. Launch of your new product onto the marketplace by licensee.

When to do it on the cheap, and when to bring in the experts

During almost every stage of commercialisation you will have the option to do it yourself, or to seek the advice and assistance of other people who have expertise in the area. Throughout this book I will try to give you information about both options. Most inventors use a healthy mix of both—doing what they can themselves because they have some skills in the area, and handing other tasks over when they haven't got a clue. Your aim is to keep your costs down, but not to jeopardise commercialisation with less than professional results. You should spend your money on service-providers who can have an important impact on your success.

Throughout Australia there are Business Enterprise Centres (BECs), and in New South Wales Innovation Advisory Centres, with professional business advisers who can provide free or inexpensive business counselling as well as some services at a subsidised rate. Most of these business advisers have also established networks with other professionals and can provide referrals, as can inventors' associations.

Almost all successful inventors seek design assistance, marketing and PR guidance, business counselling, and use the services of patent attorneys and accountants. All use commercial solicitors for the drafting of important legal agreements. Among commercial solicitors, it is wise to seek out those who have specific experience with intellectual property, something most suburban solicitors are not familiar with.

Gary McCay has some terrific advice about when to 'do it on the cheap' and when to bring in the experts. You need to decide:

- how critical a particular function is to your success;
- how complicated this function is;
- how much knowledge you have in the area concerned;
- whether you can afford not to bring in the experts in the long run.

If you decide to do it yourself and do not already have the skills, at the very least invest in a book on the subject. There are numerous user-friendly guides on such subjects as market research, starting a small business, money management, and marketing and PR for small business operators. Check the business section of your local book-store, or try your library. Small business magazines are also a helpful source of information. Each has special features and regular columns on a range of business issues that can affect inventors.

Fighting the 'inventor's syndrome'

'I am afraid my idea might be stolen'

Along with the positive attributes that successful inventors have, there is a line-up of not-so-positive features that can actually stop an inventor from commercialising his or her product concept, or that can considerably slow you down and waste precious time, money and effort.

An inventor whose air-compressor technology sets the

world standard and annually brings in six-figure royalty payments for his business based in Richmond, Victoria, calls the particular anxieties that inventors suffer from the 'greed/fear formula'. I call it the 'inventor's syndrome'. It can make the commercialisation process stressful for you, as well as for your family and friends. During the later stages of the commercialisation process, it can also make potential licensees, partners and/or investors wary and uncomfortable. All aspects of the inventor's syndrome have a positive side—they can help to motivate you and keep you enthusiastic—but they can also contribute to poor decision-making.

Worry

Right now, what you want to know is exactly what steps to take to make your great idea a reality. Naturally, you want to start making money as soon as possible. But at the back of your mind—like most inventors—you harbour the worry that someone will steal your idea or, worse yet, that someone else already has your idea and is at this very moment several steps ahead of you. You expect to see this competing product on the shelves any day now. This can be very stressful (I know because I have experienced this too). Almost every inventor I have spoken to, including the very successful, tells me that this fear is unnerving and, in its worst form, can stop you from taking any action at all. But even if someone is already working on a product similar to your invention, what can you do except follow your own path and find out for yourself whether your idea has commercial merit? And if you take your idea through its paces, it is successfully launched onto the marketplace and a competing product is also born, this may not be the tragedy you think it is.

An inventor whose product concept was almost exactly duplicated, primarily due to inadequate protection, which resulted in a competing product from Day One, told me that, although no-one likes competition, it forces you to make the best possible product to win market share. In other words, competition is healthy. In reality, very few inventions are stolen. In fact, an inventor of world-leading technology, which is now licensed for millions of dollars to major multinational companies, once told me that there were times when he didn't think he could *pay* someone to take his inventions.

Another thing that can happen if you hold your cards too close to your chest is that you isolate yourself from people who can give you valuable assistance and advice. A confidentiality agreement signed by the person or people to whom you divulge your idea will help you sleep better at night, but there are a lot of people who don't need specific details of your product in order to give you direction. This is especially true of those already in the industry or who work with, say, the materials used to make your product.

Inventors' associations (see Appendix) are often an excellent resource, and you are never required to give details of your idea there. What you will find are other inventors who are familiar with the industry, your potential consumer base, the manufacturing process, potential expenses, how to arrange a prototype or rendering, and so on.

'My great idea will make me millions!'

You may have stars in your eyes and overestimate how much you can earn from your invention. While some inventions have the potential to make it successfully to the market-place, many never see the light of day. Only a small percentage make their inventor millions. Once you have taken your invention through intensive R&D to see whether it's worth your time, money and effort, you may decide not to pursue it.

If you do decide to go ahead, you should know that self-manufacturing your product means establishing a business, and will naturally require tens of thousands of dollars—not to mention the sort of commitment of time and effort that any new enterprise of this magnitude requires. If you decide to license your idea to another party, say a manufacturer/distributor, who will take on the responsibility of making your idea a reality and pay you a royalty, you will find that most royalty rates do not exceed a small percentage of the wholesale price. Clearly, if your product's wholesale price is only a few dollars, you stand to make only cents per unit. Unless your product is sold in the hundreds of thousands, your royalty may not be enough to live on.

By the time you are in serious negotiations with a potential manufacturer/distributor, you may have already spent thousands of your own dollars, brought in investors who will require a significant portion of your profit, and taken out loans or used your credit cards to the limit (see Chapter 4). You may not make a profit or break even in your product's first year on the market, though this is an important goal. So err on the conservative side when calculating potential expense and potential profit.

'Before you know it, we'll be on easy street'

Getting a product to market will take months, perhaps years. Everyone critical to helping you commercialise your idea will appear to be sleepwalking. Because the invention is your 'baby' you will want everything to happen yesterday.

The more time you spend in the beginning taking your idea through its paces to make sure it's worth your time, money and effort, and the more you crystallise your idea into its final form (see Chapter 2), the better its chances of success. You will use your money wisely and where it counts the most. And the more complete and watertight your idea is, the more favourably it will do with investors, bank managers, potential partners and, of course, potential licensees. So take the time now to avoid mistakes later— mistakes which for many (too many!) inventors have had devastating financial consequences. Decide now whether your family home or other assets are worth losing to poor planning.

When there is a lot at stake, as with investing in a new product, most business people you approach with your idea will take their time and carefully weigh the risks against the benefits. Depending on the size of the business, the person you approach may require input from the marketing department, sales and production managers, and so on. Very rarely will there be a sense of urgency, and certainly not the feeling of urgency you will experience if time and money appear to be running out.

Along with valid assessment of your idea by people who can bring it to the marketplace, you may run into somewhat less ethical time manipulation, such as decision-makers who string you along and deliberately stall progress simply to wear you down (see Chapter 5). There is the story (now practically an urban myth) of a famous multi-national company that played a several-year waiting game with one Canberra inventor. In the end it succeeded in so demoralising the man that he eventually sold his enor-mously valuable invention at a cut price, simply to end what had become an agonising period in his life.

Another inventor found a licensee for her product towards the very end of her patent protection period (she had chosen a petty patent, which gives six years' protec-tion). She could profit from royalties only during a relatively short licence agreement with the manufacturer/ distributor because, in a handful of years, her product would no longer be covered by a patent and would be available to all comers. Though her licence agreement was certainly an achievement and she had proven her product to be worthy, she felt depressed and frustrated that it had taken so long for anyone else to grasp her idea's importance.

Of course, we have all heard about inventions that became overnight money-spinners, but I suspect most of these stories are along the same lines as actors who become overnight stars.

Last but not least: don't give up your day job. I remember two inventors who worked together at a government department and gave up their well-paid positions to pursue the commercialisation of their invention full-time. Rarely is this drastic step necessary or recommended prior to signing a lucrative licensing agreement or bringing in thousands of dollars in solid sales. In the end, these two inventors were successful—but only to a degree and nearly two years after they had left their jobs. This put an enormous strain on their marriages and finances. One sold his house and was forced to rent, the other borrowed heavily from family to keep going.

Classic mistakes made by inventors

Every time I ask inventors whether there is one thing they regret about commercialising their product, the answer is inevitably 'If only I had known then what I know now'. Had they not learned through the 'school of hard knocks', they might have saved themselves considerable time, money and effort. From my own experience, and from canvassing my panel of experts from various areas of inventing, the following are the 10 mistakes that inventors commonly make:

1. Assuming that product commercialisation is 'easy', when in fact it can be one of the most difficult ways to make a living. Financial return can take years. Not appreciating this can lead to unreasonable expectations.

2. Becoming obsessed with a new product idea at the

expense of good judgement, family, friends, paid work and other responsibilities.

3. Rushing past R&D and protecting an idea in its first, very raw form.

4. Rushing off in too many directions at once, instead of determining a specific direction and remaining focused on it.

5. Announcing a great idea to the media before protecting it, and thereby becoming ineligible for patent protection and design registration.

6. Not taking the time for education and developing new skills.

7. Contacting potential investors and licensees half-cocked, without conducting any R&D, without protection, with poor presentation and sounding like a typical 'backyard' inventor.

8. Being paranoid that an idea will be stolen and thus not seeking professional guidance from patent attorneys, accountants, solicitors, and other professionals bound by codes of ethics not to reveal inventions to others.

9. Assuming that the government will help. This is generally unfounded. In most instances financial assistance goes to established businesses with a long and successful track record.

10. Overestimating market potential and having unrealistic expectations of market share.

And you're off!

If this chapter has got you thinking seriously about what it really takes to be a successful inventor, I will have achieved my main goal. It is important that you have all the information you need to make realistic decisions and to give your great idea the best chance of success. And I don't believe in selling inventors pipedreams.

Bringing a product to market is one of the most challenging and, at times, difficult ways of making a living. It is not a hobby. In fact, product commercialisation usually resembles a small business. If you decide to self-manufacture your new product idea, as many of the inventors profiled in this book have, you are most certainly committing yourself to a business enterprise.

Pace yourself and your money. Be realistic and *relax*.

2 Turn Your Idea Into a Winner

Use R&D to save thousands and make more money

Now that you know what it takes to be a successful inventor, it is time to shift your focus to what it takes to have a successful invention. You will need to meet certain milestones to transform your idea into a moneymaker. Though it's not the sexiest term around, 'research and development' is, in my view, the most exciting stage of commercialisation. More importantly, the R&D stage is vital to your success. I can tell you with absolute certainty that if you do not conduct thorough R&D you will fail to commercialise your product idea.

There is a saying among seasoned inventors: inventing is 1% inspiration and 99% perspiration. In other words, the first great idea was only the beginning. If money were the only indicator, you would only have to look at the millions of dollars that major multinationals spend each year on R&D to see just how critical this process is to successfully launching any new product. Assuming that you can do it any other way, or that your idea is so spectacular that it doesn't need R&D, or anything else along these lines, is dangerously unrealistic.

But what does the term R&D really mean? *Research*, because you will thereby determine your idea's potential and decide to pursue commercialisation, or drop it altogether and move on. You will also use research to gain powerful supporting information to back up your idea's commercial viability, to help 'sell' it to other parties. *Development*, because you will thereby refine and evolve your idea into a winner. You will then be able to represent it in tangible form, for example as a prototype, rendering or computer animation. This is vital to helping others understand your vision, and may even be used later to initiate the manufacturing process. Finally, after thorough R&D, your product will be ready for patent and/or design registration.

Research and development are not separate activities. They happen together. For instance, as you research, you will refine and distil your idea. This may lead you to gathering further information. According to Gary McCay, every inventor should say the words 'research and development' out loud three times slowly. Why? 'Because then you might remember the word, "research". Everyone skips over this one. They see it as boring to find out what other people are doing. But it is vital', says McCay.

Shane Cavanaugh, a theatre scrub nurse, invented a revolutionary way to transfer scalpels and other sharp instruments during surgery.

THEATRE NURSE TO CHANGE WORLD PROTOCOL FOR SURGERY SHARPS

Shane Cavanaugh has been a theatre scrub nurse in Sydney for many years.

One day in theatre a surgeon asked Shane to hand him a scalpel, a request he had heard thousands of times in the past. Shane handed over the standard-issue 'kidney dish' containing the blade. The surgeon reached in and struggled to get proper hold of the scalpel. The curved shape of the dish, the surgeon's rubber gloves and the flat shape of the scalpel handle all worked against him. This combination made retrieving a blade, needle or other sharp instrument—something that happens dozens of times during each surgical operation—inefficient and dangerous.

Unfortunately, injuries from 'sharps' are all too common among surgery staff. According to Shane:

> Kidney dishes are not made for this job. They were designed for other uses entirely. But go into any hospital around the world, and you will find the humble kidney dish being used for handing over sharps. For some reason this particular incident got us to talking after surgery that day about a possible solution to this problem. In the past I have eagerly tackled some of the more technical areas of nursing, so my colleagues felt I should have a go at this.

Shane went home that day and worked with chicken wire and plaster of paris to make a prototype. It featured specially ramped sides so that the blade handle would rotate ergonomically into the hand and the blade itself was kept well away from fingers.

The prototype was trialled in theatre and was an immediate success. Shane made some minor adjustments after a few trial uses and decided to lodge his own provisional patent application. He then found an engineering firm with a computer-controlled mill and worked with the operator for several days just to input the technical specifications. This prototype cost Shane $1000, and it was put through yet another trial at his hospital. Once again, the feedback was enthusiastic from both surgeons and scrub nurses. Says Shane:

> It was becoming really clear to me that this was an important invention. To prove my feeling, I rang some of the world's most famous hospitals and spoke to other scrub nurses. All had the same problem, and all were really positive about having a well-designed solution. This cost me hundreds of dollars in international phone calls, but it was important market research.

By this point, Shane had spent around $3000 of his own money. His wife and the colleagues at his hospital were very supportive, which helped to spur him on. 'I needed guidance, though. I joined Canberra's Inventors' Association, which Andrew Holt was running at the time, and got some important direction', says Shane. He also won the association's major awards for 1996, taking out Inventor of the Year; the invention, BladeSafe™, won Best Medical Invention of the Year.

That night, Shane was approached by a representative from a conglomerate which included a medical products company. Shane and his family were put up in a hotel for a few nights so that they could talk chips. 'Although this seemed like an answer to our dreams, the negotiations went badly', says Shane. 'I began to get the feeling that this representative wanted the kudos of discovering me, but also wanted to work me out of the picture as quickly and as cheaply as possible.'

After this disappointing setback, Shane woke up early one morning and told his startled wife that he was going to Canberra and wouldn't be back until he had the money they needed to be in control:

I went to see my solicitor and said, 'I want a solution, mate. What can you do?'. He picked up the phone and that afternoon I had a meeting with a man who has access to experienced investors.

Together they set up a presentation night for investors at a local motel, complete with a mock theatre with drapes, instruments—the lot. Shane paid for one of his colleagues to come down from Sydney to help him with the presentation:

> With that scheduled, I got on the Internet and downloaded figures on the number of hospitals around the world and procedures carried out every year. We estimated conservatively how many of those procedures would be surgeries. This gave us a potential market share—also on the conservative side. And we did comprehensive costings.

Armed with this impressive supporting information, a compelling presentation from him and his colleague, and vital intellectual property protection, the night was such a success it had people literally reaching for their cheque books. 'We raised $100 000 immediately. We ended up forming a consortium which also has the security of a board of directors.'

On a high, Shane took the product to the Geneva International Exhibition of Inventions, where it was awarded a gold medal. Once again, interest was hot. It was clear that this invention had the potential to change the informal protocol for the handling of sharps in surgeries around the world.

In the end, it was decided to take control of manufacturing and distribution. An industrial designer was commissioned to make vital technical drawings. A mould is now with a Melbourne manufacturer, and finished units will be gamma-sterilised at a facility in Sydney. Shane's wife has been employed by the consortium to handle orders and general administration. 'We've set up a home office. We have a young family and my wife has always wanted to work from home. This is just one of the benefits this invention has brought us', says Shane.

As with many successful ideas, this one has opened the floodgates to other inventions: 'It is really terrific to know that I have a run on the board. I can now transfer what I have learned about successful commercialising of a new product to other ideas. It's very exciting.

Like Shane, you will probably find that there are parts of R&D you can handle on your own, and times when you will need to seek the experience and expertise of other people. Throughout this chapter and the book in general, I aim to give you information about both. Generally, seeking external help will involve paying fees, and as you can see with Shane's story you will need to be prepared to spend in the order of several thousand dollars of your own money to do it right. Unless you have already successfully commercialised a product, you will not gain finance (also known as seed capital) for your R&D efforts.

Ultimately, your goal is to recoup these expenses when you license your product idea, or when you begin to sell it if you decide to manufacture it yourself. But remember, if you are not successful you will not recoup these funds. So spend only what you can justify at each stage.

Your five goals with R&D

Your five goals at this stage and how you can make and save money are as follows:

1. Determine whether your idea is commercially viable and worthy of your commitment to spend time, money and effort on it. *Save money:* If you determine that your idea is not worth pursuing, you will not waste your time, money and effort on an idea that sounds good in theory but is not realistic.

2. Refine and evolve your idea. *Make money:* The more comprehensive your product idea is, the more money you can command from licensees, bank managers and/or potential partners and investors.

3. Translate your idea into tangible form, such as a prototype or rendering. *Save money:* When you translate your idea into a tangible form after conducting R&D, you are more likely to get it right the first time, instead of creating prototype after prototype because you discover important faults at this stage. *Make money:* A comprehensive, dynamic and professional prototype or other tangible form will enable you to command more money from bank managers, licensees and investors.

4. Put together a powerful package of information you can use to find and secure a potential licensee, or to help you gain finances, investors and/or partners. This information can also form the basis of a comprehensive business plan. *Save money:* You will have one solid and comprehensive package, so you will not be going back and forth with bits and pieces of information. This will also help to fast-track decision-making by other parties. *Make money:* You will make money because the more professional and appealing your information package is, the more likely you are to find and secure a licensee, or to gain the finance, investors or partners you are looking for.

5. Refine your idea so that you can seek intellectual property protection, such as a patent, design and/or trademark registration. *Save money:* You will save hundreds of dollars, if not thousands, simply by not seeking protection when your product is in such an early form that you will be forced to seek (and pay for) further protection later. *Make money:* You will make money because the stronger and more extensive your protection is, the

more leverage you have when negotiating royalty payments or securing investment.

Easy research and development

Here's your opportunity to transform your great idea into a product that could make you money. Remember, this is a guide only. The list is not entirely chronological: you might need to return to some points. The main R&D milestones you must meet are:

- discover your idea's potential early on;
- conduct searches, including powerful R&D with the Internet;
- familiarise yourself with other similar products already on the market;
- construct a consumer profile;
- conduct a cost analysis;
- conduct market research;
- understand market size versus market share and distribution;
- finally, revisit your product idea.

Discover your idea's potential early on

Your aim is to tap into your idea's wider potential by stepping past your initial solution to a very specific problem. Inventors tend to fixate on that first spark—but assume that this is just the tip of the iceberg. Your idea must be able to compete with products launched by businesses that have entire R&D teams *and* big budgets, not to mention a slew of already successful products.

The best way to discover your idea's potential early on is to 'play' with it, especially if this means you can use your idea in your own life on a daily basis for a couple of weeks or more. By putting your concept through its paces again and again, you are more likely to reveal new features you did not know it had. You may also discover designs of the same idea that might be just as appealing to the consumer as the one you are attracted to, and even other applications than those you had in mind initially. Clearly, this is a moneymaking exercise, because you are adding value to your end product, which will have a flow-on effect if you need to seek finance and/or investment and, of course, at the retail level by commanding a higher price.

A perfect example of the intertwining of the different aspects of R&D is that you can put your concept through its paces and be working in a vacuum if you do not conduct at least a quick Internet search of your concept to see what is already 'out there'. Even a very speedy search can include a tour of the industry, the marketplace, and an inspection of major on-line patent, design and trademark databases. This aspect of R&D can also meet up with market research, so that you enhance your final concept yet again by enabling your potential consumers to tell you what features they want, which designs they prefer, and how else they might use your product.

After searching and market research, you will want to revisit this exercise until all the elements 'gel' and your concept is fully rounded and refined. It is vital to give R&D its due, so that when it comes time to translate your concept into some tangible form it has benefited from your work, what already exists in the marketplace and the consumer's view.

I used this stage to significantly transform and add value to one of my own concepts. After my daughter was born, I wanted a quick and easy solution to travelling with her toys when I went visiting. I initially came up with a round quilt with a drawstring. I could carry her toys and provide a safe and comfortable place for her to play, no matter where I went. When we were ready to leave, I could just dump everything in the middle of the quilt, pull the drawstring, and we were off. Somehow (and I don't remember how this happened) I turned my attention to a rectangular quilt that could be folded and had handles (perhaps it was neater than the floppy, drawstring bag). One day when I was 'playing' with this concept on the floor of my lounge-room, I realised that, depending on how I folded and buttoned up the sides of the quilt, I had not only a diaper bag and a playmat but a baby-sized sleeping bag too. Although it seems obvious in hindsight (at least to me), this was an enormous revelation at the time. My jaw dropped, and I loudly announced my terrific vision to the only other person in the room—my 7-month-old baby. This discovery had transformed my '2 in 1' product into a much more valuable and appealing '3 in 1' product.

Unfortunately—and this helps to illustrate the importance of thorough and early R&D—I had fallen victim to a classic inventor's pitfall: I had already filed a provisional patent application. This new, significant addition to my product required a further provisional application, which cost me another $700, including my patent attorney's fees—money I could have saved if I had spent more time initially allowing my product to reveal its full potential.

Conduct searches

Conducting searches is one of the most universal aspects of inventing and product development. In the jargon of searching, 'prior art' is what has come before your idea and actually exists in official patent, trademark and designs databases. You are looking for inventions, designs and trademarks that are similar or identical to yours.

Of course, the main problem with searching patent, trademark and design databases is that your results can only be current to the day on which you searched. New applications are made every day. This means not only that it is important to keep your R&D current through regular 'mini-searches' but that, when you are ready to file for formal protection, say for a patent or trademark, you will need to be ready to act quickly.

Searching also involves keeping abreast of industry developments so that you know what products are already on the marketplace or are slated for imminent release, which for some reason are not represented in 'prior art'. This is especially important for those of you whose product ideas cannot be patented. You can even conduct searches on your initial idea and allow the results to spur you on to discovering your product's potential. Your goal is to ensure that your product idea goes beyond current inventions/ product ideas and that you are not working in a vacuum when there is so much information available to you. You want to avoid 'reinventing the wheel'. No matter how you search, make sure you keep records of your results and 'bookmark' all applicable Internet sites and individual pages.

Powerful R&D with the Internet

One of the most powerful ways to search these days is via the Internet. There are numerous searching facilities on-line, some of which are actually free, and others that will conduct thorough searches for you for relatively small fees. These searching facilities, such as the IBM search engine (see Appendix), will enable you to look at actual patent documents, including valuable illustrations, the name of the inventor, who the product is assigned to (usually the licensee), when the patent was filed, when it was granted, and what other related patents apply.

IP Australia, the federal government body that incorporates the Australian Patents, Trade Marks and Designs Offices, also has numerous search facilities available on its home page (www.ipaustralia.gov.au), including its easy-to-use registered trademark database. This home page has important information and links to other international search facilities, as well as to the home pages of overseas intellectual property offices, such as the United States Patent and Trademark Office (USPTO) and the World Intellectual Property Organization (WIPO).

Aside from actual databases containing official information, the Net is a valuable searching tool for finding similar products, learning about the industry and production materials, finding potential licensees and investment, keeping up with consumer trends, product marketing, home page design and much more. If you do not already have access to the Internet, make it a priority, as it is arguably the most powerful research tool you can have. There are a number of books and magazines devoted to the use of this resource that you might find helpful. The following are several universal tips to help you when searching with the Internet:

■ Use as many different search engines as possible (i.e. AltaVista, Magellan, Yahoo!) and attack the search of your idea from a number of different angles, such as:
— the concept itself,
— proposed trademarks,
— the industry,
— materials used in manufacturing the product,
— your competitors,
— directly competing products,
— patent documents,
— recognised world leaders in the field,
— on-line retail catalogues, and
— any news and e-mail groups related to any of the above.

■ Use your e-mail address to subscribe to any information sources that will come to you on subscription, such as e-mail groups and companies that offer press release subscriptions for new products and services. You will find e-mail a cheap, easy and informal way to correspond with overseas contacts, so long as your monthly server fees are reasonable. Remember, if you have access to a scanner, you can also e-mail pictorial representations of your product to potential licensees both here and overseas. But make sure your intellectual property protection is in place.

■ Almost all international intellectual property offices (IP Australia's counterparts in other countries) now have home pages on the Net. Most IP offices, like IP Australia, have on-line search capabilities of their patent, trademark and designs databases (or whatever is comparable). These home pages often have helpful links to commercial search facilities and other specialist intellectual property information.

■ An enormous number of magazines, newspapers and news services are now on-line.

■ There are specific home pages devoted to inventing, inventions (including the wacky and way-out), intellectual property protection, commercialisation, invention marketing, inventing clubs, court cases and more. Try the key words 'inventing', 'inventions', 'inventor' and 'intellectual property'.

■ The *Yellow Pages*, in particular the *Australian Yellow Pages*, is a goldmine of information for almost everything to do with product commercialisation. You can find your local inventors' club, patent and trademark attorneys, prototype services, graphic artists, market research companies, accountants, investment and more. Searching the *Yellow Pages* is easy, can be broken down into a variety of categories, including product types, business names, business types, with local, regional and national coverage (www.yellowpages.com.au).

■ Almost all federal government entities have home pages on the Internet, including the Australian Bureau of Statistics (ABS), which can be helpful in defining the size of your potential market (i.e. your product is for children between three and five years and there are *x* children in this age group in Australia). Some of these home pages also announce grants and other funds provided to a variety of businesses and organisations.

■ When a directly competing product is found on the Net, I highly recommend that you buy it or at least request any promotional material, so that you can examine your competition in detail. You might find having an account with an international express carrier, such as Federal Express, handy for getting such material quickly and with the least hassle, as these carriers also handle Australian Customs requirements. FedEx and other carriers are on the Net.

■ With so many businesses, organisations and sources of information, the Internet is, unsurprisingly, an excellent source of potential manufacturers/distributors for your idea. One potential source for US manufacturers/distributors is the Thomas Register®, a database of manufacturers of any product you care to name. Once a hefty series of books, like many resources these days it is now on-line. Membership is free (www.thomasregister.com).

■ Once your product is on the market, either through self-manufacturing or via licensing, you can use the Internet—along with other methods—to monitor your intellectual property.

■ When you do find valuable information, make sure to print out your results and 'bookmark' the page in your 'favourites' folder.

Other ways to search prior art

You can search official patent, trademark and designs databases manually and for no charge by visiting IP Australia state offices in any capital city. You can get a patent or trademark attorney to search for you, but make sure you are fully aware of their fees: searches, especially international ones, can become expensive. However, there are many inventors who consider searching to be an art, and who swear by patent and trademark attorney searches mainly because they are experts at manipulating the many search facilities available. Your patent and/or trademark attorney can follow up a successful search by immediately filing for formal protection.

Familiarise yourself with other similar products already on the market

All the successful inventors I have spoken to have told me that they consciously took time to identify what was already in the marketplace. The next best thing to the Net is getting out there and checking out the 'competition', by visiting (some say lurking in) the shops or trade fairs or, as in the case of one inventor, regional agricultural show days.

Of course, for most inventor/product developers it is usually what is *not there* that is the driving force for commercialisation. Sue Ismiel's idea sprang from her inability to find available a viable solution to her daughter's excess hair problem.

From a $5000 investment to a $7 million turnover

There could be no better inspiration for a great idea than a mother's love for her children. Sue Ismiel was desperate to find an easy-to-use, painless solution to her daughter's excess hair problem:

I tried everything under the sun—bleaching creams, waxes, even electrical devices. But it was all very painful and would have to be applied over and over again because the hair would grow back quickly and just as strongly.

Exasperated, she went into her kitchen and decided to formulate her own solution. It took 12 months of trial and error, studying current products and learning how they could be improved on. Finally, she developed a formula she and her three girls were happy with. The gel was made of all-natural, all-Australian ingredients, did not have to be heated to be used, and regrowth was finer and finer every time.

I remember lying awake the night I felt I got the gel just right. I couldn't sleep because I knew this formula would be a successful product. I had always wanted to have my own business and do my own thing. I knew this was it.

Sue offered to use the gel on a colleague and its popularity at work snowballed:

I was using the product on people at lunchtime and eventually had to make home appointments to keep up with demand. And the feedback was always terrific. Everyone who used it raved about it and felt it was superior to other products on the market.

But, like most first-time inventors, Sue was unsure of what to do next.

She went to an attorney to investigate getting a patent, but was wisely told that in her case keeping the formulation a trade secret would offer more powerful and longer-term protection. The patent attorney did, however, advise that she apply for trademark registration. She wanted to name her product Nadine, after the daughter which inspired the product, but this was already a registered trademark in the cosmetics class. They settled on 'Nad's', now a registered trademark. Sue also applied to the New South Wales Department of Health to gain approval for the product, and met all regulations needed to make the gel at home.

Sue began selling her product at the markets and eventually at shopping centres. But this was exhausting and, though the feedback continued to be glowing, Sue wondered if this was what success was all about:

> I decided to offer the formula to major cosmetic companies which did not already have a similar product. They all nodded and agreed that the product had enormous potential. But no-one was willing to take a risk.

It is possible that this was a result of the recession, because other contacts she was referred to through the Inventors' Association of New South Wales also came to nothing.

But Sue did not give up. She decided to self-manufacture and left her job with a $5000 superannuation payout. She approached her brother, an engineer, who designed the machinery she needed to move production from her kitchen. She also arranged for attractive jars, printed labels and instructions, and the right fabric strips needed to pull the gel and hair away from the skin. Eventually she also bought boxes to hold it all together: 'Once I took control of the whole process and realised that I was going to make this product a reality myself, it was really so easy.'

One day, while watching a product being demonstrated on the 'Good Morning Australia' show, it struck her that this was the ideal promotional vehicle for her. 'I make decisions instantly. I called up the producer of the show and she was enthusiastic. I paid several thousand dollars to appear with the product, which was nerve-racking, but the phones rang hot', says Sue. In fact, the telemarketing operators received thousands of orders, jamming the phone lines to the point that people began ringing Channel 10 to get their order through.

After that spectacular debut, the product sold well for some time through direct marketing. It is now sold throughout Australia through Woolworths, Big W and Safeway stores. It will soon be available through KMart and pharmacies. Its US debut will be made through a 30-minute infomercial on cable TV. This will be expanded to other direct marketing programs both in America and in Canada.

The product is a seasonal one, coinciding with the hotter months when people are more body-conscious. Tens of thousands of units are sold between September and February. Nad's® is sold at five times the rate of its competition, though it is actually twice the price.

Sue now has a plant in Kenthurst, Sydney. The business is very much a family affair. In fact, Sue's two oldest girls are now at school studying subjects directly related to Sue's vision of a wide range of cosmetic products. 'Nadine is now studying biomedical science so that she can develop and formulate other products. Natalie is studying business. And my youngest—well, Nad's can also be her future if she wishes', says Sue.

> My advice to others considering pursuing their great idea is to have a genuine product you can believe in, be persistent and don't give up. Take risks, but only ones you can support with your current resources. And avoid debt.

Sound words from a woman who has led by example.

One of the best ways apart from the Internet to keep an eye on product, industry and marketplace developments is to read trade magazines. There are hundreds of these magazines and there is sure to be one that focuses on your area of interest, no matter how obscure you think it might be.

Because you are unlikely to find trade magazines at the local newsagent (although you can ask your newsagent for a list of magazines and newsletters they have access to), your best source is *Margaret Gee's Australian Media Guide* (published quarterly by Information Australia). *Margaret Gee's* is Australia's media 'Bible' and lists all newsletters, magazines and newspapers (local, regional and national), along with TV channels, radio stations and even individual programs. You should be able to find a recent copy at your local library or you can subscribe, but this is out of the range of most inventor/product developers at several hundred dollars a year. You will certainly want access to *Margaret Gee's* later on when you begin to market your idea or seek publicity, because it includes the names of editors and their fax numbers—handy for faxing press releases at a later stage in commercialisation.

Your goals here are to determine:

- how the competing products are made, with what materials and, if at all possible, for how much;
- who makes them and who distributes them (if different from manufacturers) and, if at all possible, how much the product is sold for wholesale;
- what price point is the average for the type of product, what features make one product more or less expensive than another;
- what packaging type is used, why this packaging works or does not work, how much information about the product is given on the packaging;
- in what category these products are featured in the selling venue (e.g. at Big W your product idea may be sold in baby goods, home hardware, or small appliances);
- which features of the product appeal to consumers and which do not;
- what official requirements must be met, such as design, health and safety standards and regulations, and labelling;
- whether there is any mention of intellectual property protection, such as patent and design numbers, what intellectual property protection symbols are used on the

product itself or on the packaging, such as the registered trademark and copyright symbols (® & ©);

■ whether there are second-party endorsements common to the product type that tend to be used regularly in the related industry (i.e. organisations, celebrity or sporting identity).

If you apply this list to Sue's effort to improve on existing hair-removal products, her answers to the questions would read as follows.

■ *How are the competing products made, with what materials, and for how much?* Sue determined by trial and error most of the non-chemical ingredients of existing products by formulating her own product, and working out what she did and did not want in her formula. She was able to work out how much these ingredients would cost in bulk by contacting suppliers in her area.

■ *Who makes them and who distributes them (if different from manufacturers), and how much is the product sold for wholesale?* Sue knew who her competition was by gathering together as many examples of the product type as she could (noting distributers at this point). Later she considered cosmetic companies that might want to add this type of product to their range. Sue first sold her formula direct to the customer, and so worked out a retail price from the cost of ingredients and packaging and adding an amount for profit. When she began selling her product through other distributors, such as Woolworths, her wholesale price was a combination of her expenses, plus an appropriate profit level that would allow the distributors their own profit.

■ *What price point is the average for the type of product, what features make one product more or less expensive than another?* From her collection of existing products, Sue had a very good idea of the average price point, but her product sells at twice the average price and sells five to one over the closest competitor, simply by virtue of her marketing and distribution choices.

■ *What packaging type is used, why does this packaging work or not work, how much information about the product is given on the packaging?* The average packaging of existing products involved a cardboard box, cloth strips and a small instructional brochure. Sue later duplicated this approach by sourcing similar items from local and interstate suppliers.

■ *In what category are these products featured in the selling venue?* Sue's formula is commonly sold where cosmetic and personal grooming products are sold, which is actually a wide range of venues from discount stores to department stores, pharmacies to health food stores. Sue broke away from these traditional locations initially by selling her product through a morning television program, which features products and a hotline number through which customers can order with their credit card. The product was launched so successfully that Sue was able to sell it to more traditional retail venues, such as Woolworths. She still uses the infomercial approach, and recently used it to launch the product overseas, also with great success.

■ *Which features of the product appeal to consumers and which do not?* Sue found that women used depilatory creams because their results were longer-lasting. These products also had considerable drawbacks, and it was such disadvantages that Sue tackled with her new formula.

■ *What official requirements must be met, such as design, health and safety standards and regulations, and labelling?* Sue had to ring local health authorities to get permission to make her product from home. Sue's formula—the ingredients and the mixture—is a trade secret, so it was important to determine whether labelling requirements needed her to spell out her list of ingredients. Labelling requirements also stated that Sue must include the country of origin.

■ *What intellectual property protection applies, such as patent and design numbers, what intellectual property protection symbols are used on the product itself or on the packaging?* Noting registered trademark symbols on her collection of existing products, Sue realised that she should seek a registered trademark for her chosen name. She applied for one and was granted 'Nad's' in her chosen registration classes, but was advised by her patent attorney not to patent her formula as this would involve public disclosure. She decided to maintain it as a trade secret. The packaging does not make mention of this.

■ *Are endorsements common to the product type and used regularly in the related industry?* Sue chose not to seek celebrity endorsements.

Construct a consumer profile

Your product's consumer profile is a definition of the type of person who is *most* likely to buy your product, due to specific distinguishing characteristics, such as age, sex, financial status, hobbies/interests, employment, parenthood, and any combination of these and dozens of others. It is not enough to say that your consumer profile is 'anyone who wants or needs my product', or 'this really appeals to everyone', or 'every mother could use one'. Your product cannot possibly appeal to all people all of the time.

Establishing your consumer profile will help you refine your product idea, as it helps you to focus on this group's particular features, what they want in a product, target where or how they shop, and, more specifically, where or how they shop for this kind of product. You may also determine roughly how many people fit into your consumer group, giving you an indication of the potential market. The profile is vital to initiating market research; conversely, you can use market research to help establish your consumer profile (although this approach is usually too costly for most first-time inventors).

Your consumer profile and the data you can gather about it are important elements in your information package, and help to establish your credibility with potential investors and other people whose time and effort you require to commercialise your idea. Should you also want to market your product, you will use your consumer profile to create a targeted marketing and advertising campaign.

You probably already have a rough idea of who would want or need your product, such as the home gardener, small business people, or mothers at home with babies. You need to begin to break down this generalisation, though, by adding more features that your likely consumer would have; this is your 'core market'. For instance, your product may be best targeted at older home gardeners because it makes a particular task much easier; at small business people who export because your software program facilitates this; at mothers at home with bottle-fed babies because your product instantly heats bottles of formula.

Most products are aimed at a very specific market. My own invention, the handy bag, which transforms into a baby's playmat and sleeping bag, is clearly designed for mothers with babies. The product is also attractive to people buying for mothers with babies, almost always other women, generally older women. Over 70% of the women who buy my mini business kit (enabling them to sew and sell the handy bag themselves) live in non-metropolitan, often rural areas, are over 40 years of age, subscribe to a specific quilting magazine and tend to have school-aged children. I collect these data on my order form so that I can target my advertising and marketing materials, which helps me to maximise my budget. The consumer profile for the handy bag itself was easy, but I did not foresee the consumer profile for the mini business kit. This was revealed after it was launched through careful gathering of order form data. However, I knew enough about my most likely consumer to advertise in quilting and sewing magazines.

Designed for the baking industry, Paul Willett's robotic mixer is bought by only a small niche market, though the market itself is worth millions. Warren Wilson's blocks are aimed at a specific age-group of children. Max Moorhouse's eyewear is designed specifically for squash players. Shane Cavanaugh's sharps tray will be bought only by buyers of consumables for hospitals.

Having said that, there are some products that appeal to a large cross-section of people. John McNamee's life-saving device is useful to all people who enjoy water sports, from surfers to sailors. However, if detailed information were collected about people who bought Flube® over a six-month period or more, a pattern of the kind of person *most* likely to buy the product would emerge.

Defining a final consumer profile is not always easy, especially without expensive and professional market research, but it is essential to focusing your efforts and refining your product's appeal. It does not mean neglecting other segments of the buying audience. The following are some questions you can ask to help define your product idea's consumer profile.

■ *Who is the most likely consumer for my product?* What are some of his/her defining characteristics—sex, age, financial background, interests and education? For instance, Warren Wilson's blocks appeal to mothers of children between four and eight years, primarily aged from their mid- to late 20s to roughly 40 years of age, who have enough financial stability to be home during the day, and to have been granted and maintain a credit card so that they can order the product through telemarketing. Willie Erken's most likely consumers for his award-winning cleaning devices are people involved in the professional cleaning trade.

- *Why would someone want or need to buy my product?* Parents buy Warren's blocks as an entertaining toy for their children, also because they are perceived to be good value for money, and give children more use out of their existing blocks. Professional cleaners buy Willie's products because they make their job easier.

- *How many people in this category are in the marketplace?* The Australian Bureau of Statistics would be able to say how many children between four and eight there were on the last census, giving roughly how many parents there were for these children. For Max Moorhouse, there are x numbers of registered squash competitors in the world.

- *Where and how does my core market buy similar products?* Women mainly buy toys, like Better Blocks™, from department stores, discount chains and toy stores, and personal grooming products, like Nad's®, from their local pharmacy and supermarket. However, both these products were successfully launched on television because this consumer group was also quite happy to buy them with their credit cards while at home watching TV. Max Moorhouse i-Max® eyewear is primarily sold through mini-sports shops located in squash clubs.

- *What does this market expect of a product?* Women expect that toys will be safe, long-lasting and give good play value. People who buy gardening equipment expect that the product will be tough, sturdy, help them finish tough jobs easily, and uncomplicated to use and maintain.

■ *What is the underlying reason for someone to buy my product?* For instance, major cosmetic companies do not just sell cosmetics—they sell sex appeal, improved self-esteem, youth, glamour and so on. Other underlying reasons why your consumer may buy your product are peace of mind, status, happiness, relaxation. Buying Flube® is not only about personal safety, it's about peace of mind. Women buy the My Place® mini business kit because it offers them the opportunity to work from home, which implies more control over their life, more happiness and personal fulfilment.

Conduct a cost analysis

A cost analysis is vital, no matter which direction you take with your product idea. Your main goal is to ensure that the product can be made cost-effectively and sold at an attractive price to the consumer. If you decide to license, you will have the hard facts any potential licensee will need to know and expect of you. If you decide to self-manufacture, these figures will form the basis of your entire business and affect the amount of finance you will seek.

Networking for information

You can make this task infinitely easier by networking with contacts in the relevant industry and with people who actually manufacture products using the same materials. Your local inventors' association may also have useful contacts and information. However, according to Andrew Holt, former President of the Canberra Inventors' Association, getting the information you need can be tricky:

> There are people who are quite willing to share with you what they know and understand how you will be using

the information they give you. And there are those who think they smell a rat and will do their damnedest to keep information from you. As a result, it can take months of careful legwork to pull together all the bits and pieces of information you need to do an accurate cost analysis. But if you rush past this, you are asking a potential licensee to evaluate something that literally has no price tag. And, if you decide to self-manufacture, you cannot initiate this process without the facts.

When I designed a soft plastic identification wristband for children, my core market was the parents of children aged from two to five years. Children in this age group are notoriously mobile and easy to lose when away from home. The My Place® handy bag involved sewing and fabrics, something I knew enough about to be able to judge potential manufacturing, wholesale and unit prices. However, I knew nothing about the plastics industry—only the parameters I had set to ensure that the product was safe and effective. Based on this, I began researching food-grade plastics that could be injection-moulded and would easily take simple biro pen ink to make any writing permanent. I started by contacting the peak body for the plastics industry and was quickly referred to a list of potential plastics manufacturers. I chose a few and chatted casually with whomever I was referred to by the receptionist.

Over several days of this informal but concentrated information-gathering, I had worked out that I would need one plastic for the band, and another plastic film for the underside, on which parents would write their child's identifying information. I now knew exactly which food-grade plastic would be appropriate, bulk amounts, how much these cost, where the plastics came from and other important information. I had arranged for samples to be sent to my home so that I could test pens to ensure permanency. I later used these same networks to put me in touch with a couple of potential manufacturers. I also spoke casually with representatives from these businesses and established how much a die would cost, how much each unit would cost to manufacture, package and distribute.

Within a couple of weeks, I knew exactly how much in total each identification band would cost to make here in Australia and in Hong Kong in certain amounts (i.e. 1000, 5000, and 10 000). This unit price included all my associated costs, such as packaging, boxes, distribution—even the price of the die, amortised over 5000 units. By and large, everyone I spoke to during this exercise was happy to help, even those people who stood to make nothing from providing me with the information. It is best to assume that you will get assistance.

Lifting perceived value

Marketing, PR and packaging can have an enormous impact on how much a consumer is willing to pay for your product. The key is for these activities to add more value than they cost. For example, Sue Ismiel has retained PR and marketing experts. Although her products are primarily launched via expensive infomercials and are sold at twice the price of their competitors, they outsell these by five to one. And the Weedwakka's® packaging has gone through several refinements and a couple of graphic designers along the way, but Peter Thorne does not like to think of packaging as something that adds to perceived value—rather as a feature that elevates the product to its *true* value.

A basic costing analysis

One very basic way of conducting a costing analysis is to work backwards from the retail price. If a product retails for $30, depending on the margins that the industry works on, it may wholesale for, say, $15. Assuming that this product, depending on royalty payments and other factors, was manufactured for 20% of the retail price, it would have been made for $6, more or less. The inventor's royalty of 5% would mean a payment of 30 cents per unit sold by the manufacturer.

If you are licensing your product, you will not begin to make a profit from your royalties until all of your pre-licence commercialisation costs have been recovered; and if your royalty amounts to cents per unit, recovery could take 18 months or longer for a fairly successful product. If you are manufacturing your product, you will not begin to make a profit until you pay off your initial, up-front manufacturing and overhead costs, such as proto-typing, tooling, patent and trademark protection, or any other expenses you have incurred to date.

Through Warren Wilson's automotive business, he was able to create the tool needed for block prototypes. He churned out one block every 60 seconds, but knew that his per-unit costs would fall dramatically once the manu-facturing process was automated and plastic pellets were bought in bulk. He estimated that each block would cost no more than 1 cent to produce, and used this figure to seek investors.

ONE CHALLENGE LEADS TO 600 MILLION BLOCKS

While at the 1985 Nürnberg Toy Fair pro-moting another invention, Warren Wilson was challenged by a European toy distributor to create a block that would compete with the legendary LEGO® blocks.

At the time, these blocks essentially had a worldwide monopoly of a market worth $1 billion. Their products were protected by numerous international patents and design registrations, as well as by a famous, registered trademark.

Against these staggering odds, Warren decided to take on the challenge, and spent the next three years designing his own building block system:

> Firstly I had to work out a clipping system which would hold the blocks together firmly, yet still allow them to move. I also had to figure out what shape to make the blocks, what materials to use, and what tools and machines were needed to make the prototype blocks.

Warren had a small automotive engineering business, and it was this that kept food on the table. But eventually he began to sell off machinery to finance his efforts. He raised around $50 000 over a two-year period and funnelled this into R&D and provisional patent applications. Luckily, his machinery experience enabled him to create the machines and dies needed for prototyping. Warren's prototype produced one block every 60 seconds by hand. Today's automatic production is at the rate of 88 blocks every 60 seconds.

'I did try to get other people involved, mainly those who were already in the injection moulding industry, but I found it difficult to explain the potential', says Warren. This inability to explain that a 1-cent block represented a billion-dollar industry is something that Warren identifies as a constant barrier to investment support later on:

> After I completed development in early 1990, I began approaching people who could market, finance and manufacture the product. But no-one could see what I could see. I also feel that because the product was a toy, it was at times not taken seriously.

Ironically, Warren also feels in hindsight that he wasn't asking for enough money. He had put together an 80-page business plan with detailed costings, arriving at $200 000 as a start-up figure. 'When you're playing with the big boys, you need to speak the lingo. I think now that if I had asked for a million dollars, I may have actually succeeded, where $200 000 was just small bikkies', he adds.

Finally, in late 1991 his sister recommended he contact a friend of a friend. Kelvin Claney, a New Zealander, was in America and pioneering the infomercial format for selling new products. Warren took a big gamble, selling his last piece of machinery to finance the trip to the USA. 'It was last ditch. I had nothing left, and if I came home empty handed I would have nothing left to generate an income with', says Warren.

But Claney saw the potential and agreed to test the product on air with a $30 000 production investment. If the product was successful, he would buy the patent outright and Warren would also receive royalties. The infomercial debuted and the orders flowed in.

Since the first sales in 1992, a mind-boggling 600 million Better Blocks™ have been sold. The range is constantly being expanded by new added features, like the ability to glow in the dark and change colours. There are also accessory kits, including wheels and axles. 'We basically monitor the toy market and get inspiration to try new materials and concepts. The product is constantly being developed', says Warren. For Warren, his success is a result of sheer hard work, some skin-of-the-teeth moments, and an intense belief in the product and in his ability to make it a reality.

Warren is now conducting seminars on innovation and goal-setting. He is especially keen to get his message out to school children. 'I really love speaking to school kids because they are so full of great ideas. They know they can do great things, but they need direction', says Warren.

Along with public speaking, Warren is continuing to invent and is keen to get involved in other projects: 'I feel I am a positive and persistent person. This is pretty important if you want to succeed in inventing.'

To conduct your own costings analysis, you need to ask the following questions.

- What does it cost to manufacture (including initial costs, such as the finished prototype, tooling up, materials)?

- What distribution costs are there? Distribution costs and other related expenses, such as insurance, should never amount to more than cents per unit.

- How much will the product wholesale for? What margins are common to the industry?

- How much will it retail for? Again, what margins are common?

- What royalty will you request (5%–7% is common) and what impact will this have on the manufacturer's unit expenses?

- What sales tax applies (contact the Australian Taxation Office)?

If you are scratching your head wondering how to get answers to many of these questions, remember the value of networking. There are people in all segments of the industry, from manufacturing to retail, who will share their knowledge and experience with you as a first-time inventor. You must be creative about making these contacts and be prepared to be put off occasionally, or not have your messages returned. But somewhere along the way you will strike someone who is willing to have an open and frank conversation with you on almost anything you need to know about costing your product idea.

Conduct market research

Market research methods vary depending on the product, the inventor, the inventor's budget and the market type.

But no matter what the method, market research is absolutely essential to determining whether your product is a goer in its current form, needs more refinement, or should be dropped like a hot potato. Your goal is to get the honest feedback from potential consumers that you need to make realistic decisions, whether you intend to license or self-manufacture your product idea. The consumer profile you have already conducted will be the focal point of your market research.

Generally, market research should not be conducted without some type of formal protection, such as a provisional patent, trademark or design registration application, because it usually involves significant disclosure of the product idea. Most inventors and advisers will suggest that you back this up with signed confidentiality agreements (also known as non-disclosure forms). (Read Chapter 3 for more information on how to protect your idea and the use of confidentiality agreements.)

Max Moorhouse, inventor of i-Max® protective eyewear, tested his product with competitive squash players after provisional patent and trademark applications had been lodged. No confidentiality agreements were used because the product would be seen by the public during competitions. Players were signed up through a formal agreement and given a sample of the eyewear to be worn for every match. In a brilliant marketing move, Max also required players to wear his T-shirts whenever the eyewear was worn. At the end of the trial period, participants filled out a formal questionnaire. According to Max, this feedback was invaluable to refining his invention to the revolutionary, internationally endorsed product that it is today.

Peter Thorne, whose Weedwakka® won a gold medal at the Geneva Exhibition of Inventions in early 1998, first filed a provisional patent application and then tested his product at agricultural field days. As most country people are not shy about making their views clear, Peter is often approached by farmers who have bought his product in the past, including earlier, less refined versions of the product. Their honest, sometimes brutal assessments help Peter to continue product refinement. As Peter says, 'You've got to face the music or you are wasting your time on an expensive fantasy'.

CUTTING THROUGH THE COMPETITION

Peter Thorne is the kind of guy who won't leave a problem alone until he has solved it. He is a hands-on engineer with an impressive home workshop. So when he found that the cutting device on his new brushcutter didn't perform very well, he set about designing a better one.

Four years later, the Weedwakka® won a prestigious gold medal at Geneva, and is becoming increasingly popular with people who tackle all kinds of stubborn vegetation:

> I live in a small village near Canberra where grass gets out of control in spring. I bought a fairly heavy-duty brushcutter from my local hardware store, but quickly found that the entire product relied on a nylon cutting cord which was really ineffective, continually broke and was very frustrating to replace.

He found the alternative steel blade not much better, because it needed constant sharpening. Talking to people around town, he soon realised that everyone had the same trouble.

'It took several years of development and rigorous testing to come up with two models, which solve these problems', says Peter:

> Both have articulated blades. The steel-bladed heavy-duty model does not require any sharpening and the nylon-bladed multicut has tough, easy cutting blades that when worn out

can be replaced in seconds and without tools. Importantly, both feature a universal mounting so that you can fit them to all straight shaft brushcutters. I identified the need for a universal mounting fairly early on because this really simplifies production and marketing of the product. For safety and functional reasons, I decided not to make the Weedwakka® for the cheaper 'whippersnipper' market, but for the 'serious end' of the market where brushcutters are used by farmers, contractors, councils and the like.

This realisation helped Peter to see his solution to his specific problem as a potential money-making venture almost immediately. Patent and design registration applications were filed before the product was revealed to the public. Then, to test the market, Peter made two units and donated them to the local fire brigade fund-raising auction. Each sold for around $40. Peter then asked a friend to take along 20 units with him to an agricultural field day, where they already sold another product, the popular Gundaroo Tiller. The Weedwakka® sold out on the day. Peter decided that this product was a goer and began to make units and sell them at field days himself. 'Making and selling the units myself meant I got honest feedback from people who had actually bought my product, and from those who examined it from every angle at our stand', says Peter. 'After a few ag fairs, I would go back into the workshop. Being open to their comments has helped me to evolve the product to what it is today.'

After mark II of the product, he sought and was granted an AusIndustry R&D grant, which resulted in around $18 000. The product's packaging has also gone through several refinements and a couple of graphic designers along the way. Peter doesn't like to think of packaging as something that adds to perceived value, but rather as a feature which elevates the product to its *true* value.

One obvious aspect of Peter's commercialisation path

which is unique is his cautious approach. He realised early that his core market was the serious end of the vegetation-cutting industry, not your average home owner, and has focused his energies on this market. He did not rush into mass manufacturing of his product but chose to make and sell each unit, slowly evolving and building on each success. His products meet the relevant Australian Standards.

When he did seek finance from his bank manager, he was able to prove the product's saleability through an actual track record. 'I went to the bank and they were very enthusiastic about the product and sales to date. I also think that they were impressed that I made what I sold and was moving cautiously, but strongly', says Peter. He decided to spend $8500 to have Gledhill Belfanti Productions produce a promotional video and for Beverley Gledhill to take the Weedwakka® to the Geneva exhibition: 'I didn't hesitate to spend that money because I felt the exposure would be invaluable. But to actually win an award . . . the personal satisfaction was priceless.'

The award has brought him into contact with potential overseas distributors, and this has necessitated proceeding to the 'PCT' (Patent Cooperation Treaty) stage of the patenting process, which gives him the option to protect his product in over 90 countries. Following this stage, Peter will move to the 'national' phase and identify individual countries he would like to be protected in and pay separate patent costs for each. This is a significant financial commitment of tens of thousands of dollars.

He often used confidentiality agreements, but feels strongly that intellectual property protection is essential to have something of value to negotiate with. 'Above all, it's important to have the best possible product and capture as much of the market as I can', says Peter. According to Peter's wife, Jenny, who has experienced the entire 'adventure' with him, it's been a long, hard road, but they are beginning to see the rewards now. As we are finishing our telephone interview, I can hear Jenny whooping in the background. 'Oh', says Peter with a smile in his voice, 'it's another cheque in the mail'.

But not all inventors take the formal protection road prior to conducting market research, mainly because they either manage to get feedback without having to reveal specific features of their product, or because they are comfortable with using close family and friends as guinea pigs. For instance, Sue Ismiel, creator of Nad's® hair-removal gel, concocted her formula specifically for her daughters, and continued to test formula refinements within her family.

Other inventors avoid detailing their product's features by compiling a 'wish list' survey for family, friends and acquaintances. Participants fill out a form that asks a set of questions and then return it as feedback without the inventors ever having to reveal specific details of their idea.

Formal market research can be conducted through market research firms that specialise in gauging the appeal of potential new products from the actual buying audience. These firms can also target the most likely consumer, if you have not already conducted a consumer profile. You can find market research firms in the *Yellow Pages* under 'market research'. Certainly there are many companies in Australia and around the world that never release a product without spending thousands of dollars on formal market research. They consider this money an investment in the life of the product and an insurance policy against wasting money on a product that will not sell.

The following are some market research options.

- If you choose formal market research conducted by a specialist market research firm, shop around for the type of research that can be conducted for you, and the costs associated. In what form will your end results be provided to you? A report, graphs and tables will all be useful when compiling your information/presentation package (providing the data are favourable to your product). It is important that the firm sign a confidentiality agreement, and that, if very specific details of your product are to be revealed, anyone providing feedback for the research also signs a confidentiality agreement. You will need to decide whether or not to file for formal protection before conducting formal research. If the market research involves revealing your product in detail to large groups of people, you could become ineligible for protection later.

■ Protect your product idea as heavily as possible and conduct your own research based on the market, the product and your own skills. Use confidentiality agreements where necessary. Compile the information into some form of report for later use.

■ Limit your market research to close family and friends, making it clear that your idea should not be divulged under any circumstances. Compile the information into some form of report for later use.

If you are going to conduct your own market research, seek out the many helpful books available on this subject. Below is a rough guide to what you will need to know.

■ What does or doesn't the consumer like about your product?

■ How, in their own words, would consumers improve on or modify your product?

■ Did your product stand up to any rigorous testing that market research may have involved? Or where did it fail?

■ What would your consumers pay for the product: what is the highest amount they would pay, and are there any preferred improvements or modifications necessary before they will pay that amount?

- How would the consumer expect the product to be packaged?

- Is there any way the consumer would use your product other than the way you have presented it?

- Where and how would the consumer expect to buy your product?

- Would the consumer buy the product without being able to hold and see it?

- Does the product remind consumers of anything else they may have seen or used in the past?

- If the product is intended for both sexes, were both sexes equally comfortable with the product?

- If the product is self-explanatory or comes with information, was this sufficient for the consumer to begin using the product? Or did the consumer want to or need to ask questions? If so, what were these?

- Describe the consumer's attitude towards your product: was he or she enthusiastic, neutral, excited, interested, disappointed etc.?

Although there are a lot of questions here, try not to overload your market research participant. Choose from the above questions and decide which are the most relevant to your particular product idea. Do not avoid those questions that could result in negative feedback.

Understand market size versus market share and distribution

Market *size* is the potential number of consumers likely to buy your product. Market *share* is the number of consumers that actually buy the product. The concepts of market size and market share are where inventors can become the most starry-eyed. Whenever I hear the words 'the potential market is unlimited', or 'there are 300 million teenage girls out there who need this product', I know the inventor is not being realistic. Yes, it is important to determine as closely as possible how many people out there fit your consumer profile—mainly for the purposes of stating as much in your presentation package—but there is no chance that all consumers in your target market will buy your product.

I asked Willie Erken, inventor of the multi-award-winning Wagtail® cleaning products, to give me his opinion of the top five classic mistakes that inventors make. Three had to do with market share. He advised against 'making assumptions of prospective sales based on population size', 'anticipating taking away market share from a competitor without acknowledging . . . consumers' entrenched buying habits', and 'overestimating the actual market size, for example the size of the professional window cleaning market in Australia'. Sound advice.

Generally, only a small percentage of your potential consumer base will come into contact with your product, and even fewer will choose to buy it. One of the best ways to determine market size is to compile your consumer profile and then use the resources of a data bureau like the ABS and/or overseas counterparts of this organisation to determine the size of your group.

For instance, one of my products was aimed at children between the ages of one and five years. I contacted the ABS and found that there were two million children this age at the most current Australian census. An adviser had told me to work on the conservative notion that only 0.5% (yes, point five) of parents of this targeted age group would buy my product annually. The resulting figure of 10 000 units at roughly $0.50 royalty per unit per annum quickly wiped out my image of sunbaking on an exotic beach with a fat royalty cheque in one hand and a large mixed drink in the other.

Although the ABS was quite useful for my target market and is an excellent source of information for almost all sectors of the Australian public, there are other organisations that collect information on their specific core group. For instance, if your product is aimed at small business people, contact such peak bodies as the Council of Small Business Organisations of Australia (COSBOA) for detailed data on this group. Or if your product idea is aimed at a specific type of primary producer, contact their peak body; if you can't find it, call the National Farmers' Federation for guidance.

There are literally dozens of similar core group organisations in Australia, and they are goldmines of information. The best way to find these organisations is to search the *Yellow Pages* on-line. Whether you use the on-line service or the old-fashioned hard copy, focus on the Canberra region *Yellow Pages*, as many of these peak bodies and organisations lobby the federal government and so have their head offices there.

Distribution

Market size and market share can also be influenced by how your product is distributed. It is in your best interests to consider all possible ways of bringing your product idea to the attention of your consumer base, even if you intend to license your idea to another party which will be responsible for distribution. The more creative you are about distribution, the more likely you are to increase market share.

For instance, Peter Thorne recognised that the best way to sell his Weedwakka® was through agricultural shows. At first glance, you would say that he was limiting himself to one primary selling venue. But Peter has found from his market research that ag field days are where he is most likely to catch a good percentage of his target market, and catch them in a buying mood. Michael Beverley, inventor of the Living Picture® process for coffee mugs, can only really market his technology to a couple of companies in the southern hemisphere. He has a lucrative contract with one.

Many of the inventors in this book, including myself, are finding distribution methods that are just as innovative as our products. It is important to not assume that, because a particular product has only ever been distributed a particular way, this is the best or only way to get your product out to your buying audience. (Some more innovative ways to market new products are discussed in Chapter 5.)

Mark down all the possible places your product can be sold, such as:

- traditional venues, where similar products are already sold;
- other likely places that may not have been considered by the competition, such as an Internet home page, direct marketing and fund-raising efforts; and
- completely 'out of the square' distribution points, which seem crazy but could just revolutionise the way your product is brought to the attention of the buying audience. (Who would have thought we would now be buying books through the Internet?)

Finally, revisit your product idea

After you have taken a hard look at your product and gained vital feedback, you will most likely have gone back time and time again to refine and crystallise your product idea. I am certain that your product idea has now evolved, probably quite significantly: it should now be more realistic, more commercially viable, more comprehensive, more marketable and more likely to succeed. Before you move on to the next section, take one last look, go over your data, possibly conduct another quick search, and make absolutely sure you are ready to commit to further time, money and effort.

How to make your product idea look professional

Now that you are confident that your R&D has paid off, it is time to convert your idea into a tangible and professional form. You have a couple of choices at this point.

If you have the money, you may want to take your product idea straight to an industrial designer. These specialist designers will work with you to create polished, technical drawings. Usually these are full-colour and feature several different views. It is likely that a much-enhanced version of your product idea will result. Your industrial designer will then refer you to a prototyper to create a 3D version, unless he/she has these facilities in-house. Expect to pay hundreds, if not thousands of dollars, but the result will be undeniably cutting-edge and professionally designed, which is usually extremely impressive to potential licensees and investors.

If you choose this approach, you may wish to hold off on filing for protection until you have your final results, as the industrial designer may help you to make significant changes to your product's function and design. Though industrial designers work with hundreds of designs destined for the marketplace and are bound by professional ethics not to reveal your product idea to anyone, you may want to take along a non-disclosure form and a deed of assignment (see Chapter 3). Have a look at the Australian Design Awards Internet site to see some of the award-winning results of industrial design (see Appendix). As with Shane Cavanaugh, inventor of BladeSafe®, you may want to enter these awards at some point.

Your other choice is to take your product idea direct to any of the specialists listed below, such as a prototyper. Prototypers can provide the expertise you need to help you enhance your product idea. Once again, you may want to hold off on filing for protection and rely on non-disclosure forms and a deed of assignment.

John Levey, owner of John Levey Models and Proto-types, is a specialist in the field. Originally an industrial designer, he has roughly 15 years in the industry. He works mainly with industrial design firms whose clients are major multinationals, but he has extensive experience with inventors. Levey says that most inventors who come through his doors are bursting with genuinely good ideas, but there are also those whose idea is sorely lacking: 'The main mistake these inventors make is that they have already spent big dollars protecting a bad idea, simply because they haven't bothered to spend time in research and development.' Design is a problem for most inventors, says Levey, who risk coming off as pitifully unprofessional:

> The advice I give to every inventor is to remember that
> they are competing with companies who have entire
> professional design teams which spend months, sometimes
> years, in development. Yes, a professional prototype or
> rendering can seem expensive, but what else would you
> have a potential licensee or investor make their decisions on?

As well, Levey never proceeds with a prototype or any details of the project until a non-disclosure form has been signed. This protects both parties and is essential to the idea's security, especially as Levey agrees that seeking patent protection before the prototype is finalised will almost certainly lead to more applications down the track.

Barry Masters, owner of Barry Masters and Associates, adds: 'Please don't ask me to do the work "on spec".' While Barry is primarily an architectural model-maker, he advises that inventors seek out people who specialise in the materials the product idea requires.

Although most businesses found in the *Yellow Pages* under the model-maker category specialise in architectural models, there are a handful that specialise in new product prototypes. If you are having a hard time finding one in your area, contact an industrial designer or your local inventors' association for a reference. Fees range from $35 per hour and more for renderings (drawings) to $60 and more per hour for prototypes. As an example, Levey cites a new product for a major multinational that cost around $4500 to prototype. Obviously this prototype would have been at the upper end of the scale and of an exceptionally high quality, and might not be necessary for your purposes. But remember, after your initial prototype, amendments or improvements may need to be made, and a variety of versions can result. Ask for a quote before you commit.

The following are the five main ways that product ideas can be represented, and those you may want to contact for each if you are unable to do this yourself (use confidentiality agreements and deeds of assignment at your discretion).

■ A 3D prototype or model to scale or actual size, but not necessarily in the actual materials to be used in production (e.g. a clay or wooden model for a product that will be produced in plastic):
  — specialist model-, pattern- and prototype-makers,
  — engineering firms that specialise in the material your product requires,
  — manufacturers that already produce products from the materials your product idea requires.

■ A technical rendering of the product idea drafted on paper or via a computer-drafting program, possibly one 3D type view or separate views of each side of the product:

— industrial designer,
— draftspeople,
— graphic and commercial artists.

■ A computer animation of the product:
— specialist computer-animation firms.

■ If your product is a formula of ingredients, a sample of the formula:
— industrial chemists familiar with the ingredients your product idea requires.

■ A comprehensive written description and/or a shorter summary, which will supplement the above choices:
— professional writer.

Once you have the final form of your product idea, you must consider intellectual property protection. For those of you whose idea cannot be protected by a patent, which protects function, you should seriously consider applying for a design and/or trademark registration. You want the maximum protection for the minimum outlay. You will also need a confidentiality agreement (non-disclosure form), and there are standard forms available from many commercial solicitors, or one can be drafted specifically to meet your needs.

Once protection is in place, you can move on to conducting formal market research and creating your winning presentation package.

Creating a winning presentation package to help sell your idea to others

You have now completed the R&D phase and have some form of intellectual property protection. It's time to pull it all together into a comprehensive and relatively standardised package you can use to sell your product idea to others. This package can include a business plan or be integrated into a business plan.

According to Beverley Gledhill, Australia's Ambassador to the Geneva Exhibition of Inventions, who has presented hundreds of inventions on TV and radio, a lack of professionalism can kill a great idea. Says Beverley:

> If you remember that your main competition is probably a multinational with millions to throw at new ideas, then you will carefully consider how you present yourself and your product. Inventors often find it difficult to take an objective look at their product concept. They usually provide too much detail, usually technical details, and forget that they have just seconds for their product to impress.

Your goal is to create a package that not only sells your idea but establishes your professionalism and seriousness. You do not want to be branded a 'backyard inventor'—you want to be viewed as a 'product developer' or small business person. This package will obviously be very helpful for interstate or overseas contacts, but it is also recommended for contacts in your area. You can use it to initiate discussions, or as reference material that can be left for consideration after your meeting.

Always make contact with the person you have targeted to receive your package so that you can briefly introduce yourself and your wish to forward them some information about your product idea. Ensure that they are willing to sign a confidentiality agreement and send this on for signing. Once it is received back fully signed, you are free to forward them your package.

The following are some points to consider when compiling your package.

- You can create your own professional-looking stationery on a computer (if you don't have this kind of stationery already) that has a simple address block at the top of the page which is centred or placed to the left and states your name, address and any contact phone numbers. Keep it simple: no fancy fonts, just Times Roman and no larger than 14–16 points.

Alternatively, scan into your computer a professional, appealing photo of yourself (nothing else will do). Reduce it to no larger than 4 × 4 cm and place it in the top right-hand corner of your letterhead template. You may want to put a text block under your photo in roughly 7–9 pt type stating your name and the title 'Product Developer'. Place your address block, roughly the same size and in Times 12 pt, in the top left-hand corner of this page. Placement of your address and photo blocks are within the normal top-of-the-page margins of your word-processor's standard settings.

- Write to the person you have targeted using your letterhead. The letter should include (see sample letter on the next page):
  — your thanks to the person for their time and willingness to consider your product idea for the purposes of, for instance, potentially adding this product idea to their product line, or gaining finance or possible investment;
  — an outline of the attachments you have included to help illustrate this product, such as fact sheets, photos, renderings;
  — a mention that you will be in touch within a few days to talk further and/or a reference to your contact numbers should they want to contact you before then.

- Your R&D will by now have curtailed your temptation to make grand, unsupported statements; however, you should have a title page to follow your letter which clearly states the benefit to the reader (i.e. 'How your

Alicia Beverley
Product Designer
Address
Telephone number
Facsimile number
E-mail address

Alicia Beverley,
designer of My Place®,
'The handy bag that's a
playmat and sleepingbag too!'

Mary Smith
Director
New Products Division
Company Pty Ltd
Address

9 April 1994

Dear Mary,

It was a pleasure to speak with you last week regarding
My Place®, my new three-in-one baby product. Thank you
for your time and willingness to evaluate My Place® as a
potential addition to your company's product line.

To assist you with this evaluation process, please find enclosed a
comprehensive information package, comprising the following items:

- a press release from the Canberra Inventors' Association
  announcing my recent awards for Inventor of the Year
  and Invention of the Year (Consumer Category);
- a fact sheet which includes a brief summary of the
  product, compelling market research, an in-depth costing
  analysis, and a brief outline of the intellectual property
  protection that supports this product; and
- a colour photograph of each of the product's three
  modes: handy bag, playmat and sleepingbag.

I understand that you will take My Place® through your own
detailed evaluation process, and I would appreciate regular
contact with you so that I can follow my product's progress
and answer any questions that may arise. As such I will be in
touch with you in the next few days so that we can speak further.

Kind regards,

Alicia Beverley

business will profit from X'). This title can be changed depending on the potential reader; for instance, the title you use for a bank manager will not be the same as one used for a potential licensee.

■ Determine your main categories of information (as per those outlined in the R&D section) and create a brief, easy-to-read table of contents giving page numbers, or a brief line-up of bullet points if your information is contained in one fact sheet.

■ Prepare a fact sheet or a series of fact sheets with clear, bold headings which relate to your table of contents, and which contain well-spaced, relatively short paragraphs (usually no more than three related sentences each). Make sure to start your fact sheet or sheets with a non-technical, jargon-free summary of your product.

■ Make sure you include a shortened version of your intellectual property portfolio that includes the intellectual property assets you have and the protection that applies.

■ If you have a special announcement to make, such as an award or endorsement from an important individual or organisation, write a press release, and include this as well, either before the table of contents page or just after.

■ If you have produced a 3D prototype you may want to have professional (or at least professional-looking) colour photos to include in this package; make sure to identify these photos as an attachment in the table of contents.

■ Include copies of your rendering or a copy of your computer animation tape; also refer to these as an attachment in your table of contents.

- Include a business plan document only if the presentation package is being used for gaining finance or investment.

Although this sounds like a lot, it should really only be a few bound pages, as follows:

- a one-page letter;
- one cover page with title stating the benefit/s to the reader;
- a one-page table of contents;
- a one-page media release (if appropriate);
- one to three pages of fact sheets (you can always supply more detail if requested to do so);
- a one-page intellectual property portfolio in bulleted list form;
- attachments as necessary, such as renderings or a business plan (if the package is being used to seek finance or investment).

Secrets to using the media

The media can be a great tool, or it can be your enemy and your undoing. For inventor/product developers, media success or failure has a lot to do with timing. Never approach the media before you have established which intellectual property rights you will use to protect your idea.

In Australia, if you reveal your product idea to the public through an article or news story, for instance, your product immediately becomes ineligible for patent protection and design registration. It's that serious. But time and time again I have seen over-eager inventors immediately ring their local paper or television station to announce their breakthrough to the world.

The time to go to the media is when protection is decided and in place, and when you are ready to reveal your product idea and/or have a specific announcement to make. It may be best to hold off going to the media until you have a specific announcement, such as a licensing agreement, award or important endorsement, or you are about to begin production or distribution. You may not get a second chance after your initial, 'this is what I've invented' announcement. If you decide to wait, you should consider media usage in combination with other public relations and marketing efforts. If these are being handled for you by a service-provider, work with them to establish an overall media/PR/marketing strategy.

If you want to announce before then, or if you will be handling the media on your own, the following are some useful tips.

- Your local library should have a copy of *Margaret Gee's Australian Media Guide*, considered the Bible of the media industry. It lists every media outlet, including contact names, and is invaluable to targeting your preferred media coverage.

- Try to think of your invention in terms of the 'story' it represents to a journalist. What's the angle—what's interesting about what you have to say? How will it affect people's lives?

- When you are ready, you may want to contact:
  — your local radio and TV stations,
  — popular press magazines (*New Idea*, *Women's Weekly* etc.),
  — your local newspaper,
  — national publications, especially those oriented towards small business and the retail trade, if this applies,
  — trade magazines, especially those which focus on the type of materials or manufacturing process your product idea uses; *Manufacturers Monthly* has a

regular section featuring new products and manufacturing processes.

■ To make contact you can fax your press release to the
editor or to a specific journalist. But make sure you can
be reached immediately, otherwise they will quickly
move on to another story. Have your information package handy in case more detail is requested.

■ The following are the main elements of a successful
media release (also see sample release):

— a beginning paragraph which states the award or other
significant announcement, or the breakthrough,
invention, innovation, new product etc. ('John Smith
today announced that he has solved the worldwide
problem of tangled computer wires forever with his
breakthrough invention, The Untangler™');

— a few quotes from yourself about how you developed the invention, what applications there are and
why people will want or need your invention;

— whether you have had interest from a manufacturer;
if you won't jeopardise your negotiations and relationship with this business, you can include details
about how you are working together to bring your
product to the market;

— your contact details, especially a mobile or a phone
number at which you are immediately available;

— if you need to have your press release coincide with
a particular event, make sure to put the words,
'Under Embargo' in the top right-hand corner along
with the time and date before which the release
cannot be used. So if your event is at midday on
7 September, it will read: UNDER EMBARGO
until 12 pm, 7 September;

— your copyright notice at the bottom in smaller print
(e.g. ©1999 Your Name or Your Business Name.
All rights reserved).

MEDIA RELEASE

Under embargo until 9 am, 24 October

Canberra Inventor of the Year Announced

The Canberra Inventors' Association has announced Ms Alicia Beverley as Canberra Inventor of the Year 1994 and one of her products as Canberra Invention of the Year 1994 (Consumer Category), at its recent awards night.

Ms Beverley, a product designer and public relations consultant, developed the winning invention after the birth of her daughter three years ago.

Essentially a specially-shaped quilt, My Place® — 'a handy totebag that's a playmat and sleepingbag too!' — goes on sale in Australia next week.

A major American company has bought the rights to the product for North and South America, and the product will be available in department stores and boutique baby shops across America by mid-September.

Of her double award, Ms Beverley said: 'I am absolutely thrilled to be recognised by my peers and named Canberra Inventor of the Year. From the moment the proverbial light flashed in my mind to actually seeing my product on the shop shelves has been one of the toughest, and yet one of the most rewarding times of my life. But there is a tremendous difference between simply inventing and actually commercialising your product. The key is responding to the market in novel ways, knowing how to market your product *and* yourself and, of course, persistence and sheer hard work.'

Her second and third inventions are now being considered as potential promotional products by major companies all around the world.

'I promised myself that I would not pursue further inventions until My Place® proved itself successful. It has, and now I have high hopes that my subsequent products will become just as popular', she said: 'All the hard work has paid off, and now my ideas are my business.'

For more information, contact: Ms Beverley on (02) 6000 0000.

3 Protect Your Product Idea

Intellectual property rights for non-rocket scientists

Intellectual property (IP) is one of those unfortunate terms that immediately makes one think of scientists in white lab coats conducting experiments that will lead to major, world-changing breakthroughs. But in fact intellectual property is simply any original idea that is unique to you—even if your idea is not new but is an improvement on someone else's idea.

What are intellectual property rights?

To gain protection over your idea, it must be expressed in some tangible form. You cannot protect a mere 'idea'. Thus Warren Wilson could not protect his concept of interlocking blocks. However, he could protect any drawings of the blocks (copyright), prototypes (design registration/ copyright), the product itself (patent/design registration), any machinery designed for making the blocks (patent/design registration/trade secret), drawings of this machinery (copyright), plastic formulas for the injection-moulding (patent/trade secret), the product's trademark (registered trademark), and promotional materials such as brochures, photographs and a presentation package (copyright). All of these constitute Warren's intellectual property assets and the intellectual property rights that might apply.

Intellectual property rights—patents, trademarks, designs, copyright, circuit layout rights, plant breeders' rights and trade secrets—give you a legal and official monopoly over different aspects of your product idea in the country in which they are available. To gain the most powerful protection for your entire range of assets, you would use a matrix, or combination, of intellectual property rights, such as a patent, design and trademark registrations and copyright.

Some of these rights are gained automatically without having to apply for protection: these are copyright, circuit layout rights, trade secrets and non-registered and non-registrable trademarks. The rest—patents, registered trademarks and designs, and plant breeders' rights—must be applied for and granted officially by the appropriate government body. You can apply for all of these rights yourself and pay only official fees, which are usually quite low. However, you will be responsible for:

- tracking your application through the system;
- providing counterarguments, answering queries and demands for more information from IP Australia examiners; and
- being aware of all anniversary dates on which official fees become payable, or protection will be lost.

If you have the finances, your other option is to seek the services of a reputable patent or trademark attorney—especially for patent applications, which are very complex and time-consuming documents to prepare. A good local patent and trademark attorney is vital when filing overseas for patents, trademarks and designs.

IP Australia is the federal government body that incorporates the Australian Patents, Trade Marks and Designs Offices. Plant breeders' rights are granted by the federal Department of Primary Industries and Energy. Issues having to do with copyright and circuit layout policy are handled by the federal Attorney-General's Office (remember, you do not have to apply for copyright). All of these organisations have their main offices in Canberra, but IP Australia has a network of capital city branch offices in which you can apply for rights, search databases free, access some library resources and generally ask non-advice-related questions about patents, trademarks and designs.

IP Australia has a useful home page on the Net (www.ipaustralia.gov.au), where you can search databases, download forms, learn more about the entire range of intellectual property rights, access links to other helpful sites, as well as examine a few examples of famous Australian patents, trademarks and designs. IP Australia also has a range of free information kits for patents, trademarks and designs, which include applications, eligibility requirements, fee structures and other details. These will be posted out to you free of charge. I recommend calling now and getting each and every free kit so you can start your own intellectual property resource library. Your local branch of IP Australia can be found by calling the telephone information operator or through the *White* and *Yellow Pages*.

Which rights you should use for the best protection

Registered and non-registered trademarks

Along with all the blood, sweat and tears you have invested, you may have come up with a snappy new name for your product idea. For some inventors whose product idea is not patentable, a design registration and a registered trademark may be the only protection available. Even though your product idea may eventually be licensed to a company that will take responsibility for final development, having a trademark will generally add value to the overall package you are offering. This asset could lead to a higher than usual royalty payment.

Self-filing for trademark registration in Australia is relatively easy and cheap, or you may opt to use the services of a trademark attorney.

The facts

A trademark can be a letter, number, word, phrase, sound, smell, shape, logo, picture, aspect of packaging, or any combination of these. A registered trademark is formally registered with a national intellectual property office (e.g. IP Australia) and, in this country, you can register your trademark within 42 specific product and services categories, known as classes. In general, registered trademarks cannot be descriptive of your product or service (Bob's Tyres) in the class in which you are registering, make claims that could also be made by your competitors (Bob's Best Tyres), or involve geographical or common first names (Gold Coast Tyres). However, every year I see registered trademarks which break a few rules, and some which seem to have merit but are knocked back. The best thing is to choose a unique, simple trademark which has its own appeal.

When you do apply for a registered trademark, the date on which your application is accepted is called your 'priority date'. This is the date from which your ownership of this intellectual property is officially documented. When your registration is successful (usually within only a few months of application), you will be given an official registration number.

If you choose to apply overseas, Australia's involvement in international treaties means you can use this priority date in your overseas applications within six months of your Australian filing. So if you have filed on 7 June 1998 in Australia, and then choose to file in America four months later (in October), you can use 7 June as your ownership date.

So long as you pay your registered trademark's official fees every 10 years, it can be maintained indefinitely. After you have applied for registration, you may use the TM symbol next to your mark. When you gain registration, you may use the ® symbol. Make sure you use these symbols consistently every time your trademark appears.

If you apply for registration and are knocked back, this is not the tragedy it would appear to be. If you cannot gain registration, then no-one else can. And so long as you have documented your use of the trademark and you are the first to use it, your trademark has a strong measure of protection. Not all trademarks are registrable, such as the Australian Airlines mark, which is obviously too descriptive in every way. However, it is a valid trademark and was valuable at the time it was in use. Copyright is not considered sufficient protection for trademarks.

Do not apply for trademark registration before searching IP Australia's trademarks database, available free on-line through its home page and through state offices. And do not use graphic design services until this search has been conducted. You will save time and money by not committing to a trademark that is already registered by another party in the class or classes you need protection in. Once you have conducted a search, and you find that your preferred mark is available, apply for registration immediately (remember, a search is valid only to the day on which it is conducted, as new applications are received every day).

How the inventors in this book did it

The following is some interesting background for a few of the trademarks featured in this book.

Wagtail® cleaning products. Willie's wife came up with the name during a brainstorming session: 'Wagtail. You know, like Willie Wagtail. The fan on the bird's tail.' The trademark and the ® symbol denoting it as registered are now used on the product itself, in advertisements, on business cards and so on. The TM symbol is used on the main phrase that consistently accompanies their logo: 'The pivotal change in cleaning.'

My Place® 3-in-1 baby product. I named my product 'My Place' because it was a baby's place to sleep, rest and play. I registered that name fairly early on, and it is now an important, personally owned asset that I license to my company.

Nad's® hair remover. Sue had wanted to name her product 'Nadine', after the daughter who inspired the product. As this was already a registered trademark in the cosmetics class, Sue settled on the name 'Nad's', which she has now successfully registered as a trademark.

Living Picture® sublimation process. Although Michael Beverley did not consider himself savvy about intellectual property matters when he first began R&D for an important new sublimation process, he did know the value of a registered trademark. Michael wanted a trademark that would convey the brillant, lifelike colours that his process could achieve, and hit on 'Living Picture', now a registered trademark.

Flube® life-saving device. John McNamee actually wanted to call his product 'Flotation Tube', but this was too descriptive to gain registration in Australia. However, Flube® is a clever, memorable trademark, and makes a good front for his product.

To save a drowning man ...

Imagine you are are going up a glassed lift which overlooks the ocean. You look down and see, to your horror, that a man is drowning. There are no lifeguards on the beach. John McNamee, inventor of the life-saving device Flube®, says: 'It was awful to be so powerless, but my wife and I realised later that, even if we had been standing on the beach, we would have been just as unable to help the man.'

Like John and his wife, few people have the skills and strength needed to rescue another person, especially in the surf. 'So often the person who goes to the rescue becomes a victim themself. You don't want to be a hero when the chances are neither of you will make it', John adds.

According to John, skill and strength are often not essential anyway, as 95% of drownings occur within only 2 metres of safety:

> The answer is 'reach or throw'. You need to be able to reach or throw to the drowning person something which can help them stay afloat. Of course, the standard orange life-saving ring is not something the average member of the public packs with them for a day at the beach. And many households don't even have one for the pool.

John, a retired engineer who has invented other products in the past, couldn't shake off his tenth-floor view of a tragedy in the making. He began to consider a product that could not only be used by another person to save someone from drowning but was compact, lightweight and cheap enough to actually be worn by people enjoying water sports. The majority of current life-saving devices are designed specifically to hold the head up. John kept looking for an improvement on this concept, but found he wasn't getting anywhere. Finally his son advised him to 'stop trying to be 100% perfect. Just design something that is simple and easy to wear'.

Within 20 minutes John had the answer: a 6-foot tube with a 4-inch diameter with handholds at each end. When extended with one arm to another person reaching out for it, the distance covered is over 3 metres. The tube could also be velcroed together to form a buoyant circle, which you can hang onto or circle around your body to provide lift under your arms.

The entire tube fits into a small pouch, much like a bumbag, and can be worn on the hips. When a cord is pulled, a small gas cylinder completely inflates the tube within two seconds—clearly an enormous improvement on existing devices, which are too awkward and bulky to be used consistently.

'At first we called it "Floating Tube", but this is too descriptive to gain trademark registration. Flube was just one of those perfect flashes of inspiration', says John. Recognising that it would be critical to success, John arranged for Flube® to be trialled by the Royal Life Saving Society of Victoria. It was almost immediately used by a life-saver to rescue two little boys. According to the life-saver there had been no time to get out the boat, or to run back to base for any devices, but he was actually wearing Flube®. The life-saver called it a '100% perfect rescue'.

Flube® is now endorsed by the Worldwide Life Saving Organisation. Though the product seems destined to succeed, John has experienced his fair share of bureaucratic frustration with the official standard for life-saving devices, as his device sets a precedent and does not fit any of the existing categories. According to John, 'It's frustrating, but the endorsements the product has gained so far speak for themselves, and are just as important to establishing credibility'.

John has used his personal finances to fund patent applications in over 40 countries, worth tens of thousands of dollars. He has also chosen to self-manufacture and distribute the product, and is currently researching distribution and marketing options, with a view to having the product available through department stores. It should retail for around $50, which makes it the cheapest life-saving device on the market.

His main challenge is focusing people on the need to have a life-saving device. 'Complacency is a killer. People die simply because they are unprepared. With Flube® there is no longer a reason not to have a life-saving device at hand', says John.

Patents and patentable material

For many inventors/product developers, a patent is the most powerful form of protection for how an invention functions. The function is often supported by dynamic design elements, and these may be protectable by a design registration. This combination has often provided watertight protection. Together with a registered trademark, a powerful matrix of protection is created. However, not all new product ideas are patentable—especially those that do not involve an inventive leap but are more a new design for existing technology. For instance, in the case of an exciting new mobile phone shape to house existing, patented electronics, design registration becomes vital.

In certain industries a patent is the only recognised and acceptable form of protection; certainly most investors, bankers and potential licensees feel more comfortable about risk-taking when a patent has been granted, or at least an application filed.

The trade-off with patenting is that details of your

invention will be published and placed in the 'public domain'. This can trigger competitors to improve on it or find a way around it. If your patentable invention is released to the public before you apply for a patent—say through a press release, news story, advertisement or trade show—you will have lost eligibility for patent protection. This is not the case in the USA, for instance, where you have a year from public announcement to file for a patent application (as this could change at any time, consult the US Patent and Trademark Office for updated information).

Some inventions, particularly new manufacturing processes that will never be marketed to other parties and are unlikely to be reverse-engineered (figured out by working backwards from the final product), are not patented but are kept 'under wraps' through a trade secret.

The facts

A patent is a formal nationwide monopoly granted by a national intellectual property office (e.g. IP Australia). A patent protects a new or significantly improved invention, manufacturing process, original computer software, chemical or genetic formula (not including new plant breeds). There are two kinds of patent—petty and standard—and two ways of applying for patent protection—provisional and complete specifications.

Standard patent protection lasts a maximum of 20 years, petty patent protection a maximum of six years. A provisional patent application is a shorter, less complex document than a complete specification. It is used to quickly establish your ownership and commence the patenting process. If your product idea undergoes a major refinement, you can file another provisional specification, and this, plus any earlier applications, can be combined into your final complete specification.

As with trademarks, the day IP Australia accepts your

application is your 'priority date'. Australia's involvement in international treaties means that you can use your priority date when filing overseas during a specific time period. From your provisional application's priority date, you have 12 months to file a complete specification. This period is helpful for determining the commercial viability of your invention and whether or not to take on the further expense of a complete petty or standard application.

Once you have applied for protection or been granted a patent, make sure to crow about it so that your competitors will back off. Apply the words 'patented', 'patent pending' or the actual patent numbers to your product, packaging and promotional materials.

Contact the state office of IP Australia and have it send you its patent kits—a standard information kit including an application form, and another kit which helps you to self-file. Both outline patent eligibility issues and patent application and filing fees. The kits also detail the special timing that applies to patenting in other countries. IP Australia has produced an inexpensive CD-ROM about patenting, called 'Protecting your edge with patents'. IP Australia staff are very helpful and willing to discuss specific details about patenting. However, they will not advise you as to whether you should or should not patent.

Patent expenses and timing, especially when you want to file in other countries, can get very complex. I highly recommend that you ask your patent attorney to lay this out on paper for you to refer to later.

How the inventors in this book did it

Expanda-Stand® brochure holders. Peter Eaton's product is an excellent example of creating a matrix of protection around a central patent. Says Peter:

> If you want to exploit something commercially, you want
> to send it out into the market with whatever formal

protection you can afford. In my case, this has meant a patent to protect the unique way in which my brochure holders interlock with each other to create a tailored display; design registrations to protect the unique way in which they wrap around the full height of the brochure without obscuring your view and other key design aspects; and, of course, a registered trademark for Expanda-Stand®, my frontline into the marketplace and a powerful marketing tool.

WHY ONE DILAPIDATED HOTEL IN THE MIDDLE OF NOWHERE MEANT SO MUCH

It was on the way back to Johannesburg from a stay in Kruger National Park that Peter and Veronica Eaton and their two young girls stopped off in the town of Belfast. They were in the middle of a violent electrical storm. Their only immediate option was an old hotel that had seen better days. Veronica Eaton thought the place looked so run down that it would be best just to use the facilities and get a snack closer to Johannesburg.

They parked the car, ran into the hotel's reception area as quickly as they could to avoid the driving rain. The place was dark, dingy and depressing, but it held a fantastic discovery. There, bright and shiny in a place of prominence, was Peter's award-winning brochure holder from his range of display products, designed in South Australia's Clare Valley. 'It was a terrific feeling. The sort of moment that all inventors live for', says Peter. The incongruous experience highlighted just how far Peter Eaton had come with his invention since a Clare Valley businessman first came to him with a cry for a better brochure holder.

Peter has a long history of successful innovation, including inventions for towing, suspension and safety equipment for caravans and mobile homes. At the time of the request, his steel fabrication business was manufacturing products of his own design, such as grape bins and decorative garden arches—feeding on the more traditional aspects of life in the Clare Valley, the home of some of the world's finest wines. But, like so many others, he was struggling through the recession.

Within minutes one day, Peter had quickly knocked together a metal stand that overcame the businessman's brochure display problems, even going a few steps further. Though his range is now made of tough styrene, the basic design remains the same.

Peter decided to take part in the Enterprise Workshop, a nationwide program which began several years ago as a wholly government-run initiative but which is now only partially funded by federal and state governments. Today, it is run as a commercial concern by private licensees in each state and territory. Depending on the location, participants pay from $3000 to $4500 to take part in the six-month intensive program. Through a team format, participants choose a particular product or service idea and learn the practicalities of turning that idea into a commercial reality. Their R&D and resulting business plan is of the calibre necessary to actually seek finance and establish a business.

In Peter's case, he worked in a small team that chose to focus on his stand concept. He had already applied for provisional patent and design registration applications through his patent attorney. At the end of the program he took his business plan to the bank and was granted a loan. He used these funds to launch production and commission the marketing tools he needed. That was in 1990. By 1993 Peter had begun to export, the next year winning the South Australian Chamber of Commerce's New Exporters Award.

Expanda-Stand® products are now made in Australia, as well as overseas, and are sold throughout the United States, the United Kingdom, Europe, Asia, South Africa, New Zealand and Australia. And usually in nicer environments than the dilapidated hotel they encountered during their African trip.

According to Peter, once he started looking into the size of the brochure-holder market, he was amazed at the sheer scale:

> If you think about it, just about every business, organisation and institution produces brochures. And most often, these displays look awful—not the professional image you would want to project—with brochures flopping over and the stand cumbersome and usually very unattractive. I made it my goal to make the best possible display system.

For Peter, making a living out of his invention goes hand in hand with understanding his intellectual property rights:

> Whenever your livelihood relies on new products, you are going to worry how long you will have in the marketplace before cheaper, lesser-quality imitations start popping up. But intellectual property rights tend to hold your competition at bay for much longer than if you had no protection at all. Then it would simply be a feeding frenzy.

> One of the obvious advantages of successfully commercialising his invention is the lifestyle it has given Peter and his family: 'I love the Clare Valley. To be able to export my product to the world from paradise, well, what more could you ask for?'

Universal™ power track. John Sinclair conducted some informal market research by showing rough sketches of the original power track to a handful of electricians. After their extremely favourable response he decided to file his own provisional specification. Says John, 'When I look back at that application now, I have to laugh. It was more my life's story than a summary of an invention'.

Wagtail® cleaning products. Willie Erken took part in the New Enterprise Incentive Scheme (NEIS) program, where participants form teams centred on a new product or service idea and develop a workable business plan. His team chose to focus on his prototype pivoting window cleaner. Halfway through the business plan process, Willie discovered the central, innovative element that makes his products unique. Literally the next day, Willie filed a 'provisional' patent application through his patent attorney because he felt strongly that he must move immediately to provide his idea with protection—certainly before it was revealed to the rest of the NEIS team.

C'aireCush®. Joan Stuckey has not one but *three* highly successful products on the world market. Units have sold in the hundreds of thousands and brought in millions of dollars in revenue. Joan's first patent, filed 30 years ago, was so important that she was tracked down by her potential competitors and paid handsomely for it. Many years later, Joan patented the C'aireCush® cushion. This led to two other related products, also now patented.

PATENTLY OBVIOUS SUCCESS

When I went looking for Australian female inventors to supply case studies for this book, a contact of mine gave me Joan Stuckey's telephone number, saying something about a cushion she had invented. For whatever reason I put the number aside for some weeks. As the book neared completion, it disturbed me that I had been unable to locate no more than one successful female inventor. Then I remembered Joan. I rang for an interview only a few days before the manuscript was due in, and was astounded by her story.

Joan has won over half a dozen significant national and international awards—from Australian Inventor of the Year to the World Intellectual Property Organisation's gold medal. She has been featured widely throughout the media in articles, radio interviews and TV programs.

The C'aireCush® exercise and support cushion is Joan's central product—a simple, fan-shaped cushion with two air chambers. As your feet pedal or treadle, air moves from one chamber to the next. It is an easy but effective exercise which helps to relieve swollen legs and feet by promoting blood circulation. Says Joan:

> In the late 70s I began to notice a number of articles about DVT—or deep vein thrombosis—suffered by people making long air or coach journeys. Aside from the discomfort of swelling legs and feet, DVT can actually cause life-threatening blood clots, so the problem can be a serious one. I believe in low-cost, appropriate technology. People who are travelling need something lightweight, easy to use and unobtrusive. So nothing but a very simple solution to this problem would work. An inflatable cushion struck me as ideal.

Joan patented the cushion and applied for a registered trademark for the name, but it quickly became apparent that Joan's 'less is more' approach had resulted in a product with dozens of other applications, especially within the medical and health-care fields. Says Joan, 'Next thing I knew, the C'aireCush was being trialled, and then gaining widespread popularity in hospitals for postsurgical patients, pregnant women, people with diabetes, arthritis and kidney problems, among others'.

Along with numerous applications, Joan's concept led to two other related products. The first was a pressure-distributing seat, designed to fit standard wheelchairs but also very popular with cabbies and others who are confined to their car for long periods. Then came the pressure-distributing mattress overlay, which reduces the risk and severity of debilitating and painful pressure sores. Says Joan:

> Both of the subsequent products resulted from people using the original cushion to solve other problems. For instance, people confined to wheelchairs were sitting on the exercise

cushion, leading me to design the seat cushion. Doctors rang me to say that cancer patients were taking the seat cushion into cancer wards because their weight loss had made them vulnerable to pressure wounds. The mattress overlay was an obvious next step.

Joan applied for two new patents. To date, her intellectual property protection costs around the world have reached the $250-million mark.

Now, of course, with patents, design registrations and registered trademarks in so many countries, my intellectual property expenses are staggering. But I have always believed that a product has to pay its own way. At 55, when I invented C'aireCush, I had my own finances to draw on, but I restricted my commercialisation expenses to $5000.

Publicity from her various awards on radio and especially on major television shows featuring Australian inventions, such as 'What will they think of next?', gave the products an enormous boost. Sales would always shoot up after each show. Says Joan, 'I really gained publicity that I could never have afforded. I was very lucky'.

Joan never wanted to be burdened with a sales force and the headaches that can accompany this kind of enterprise. Instead, she has distributors around the world. Joan receives an order, faxes it to her manufacturers in Japan, and the goods are dispatched. It's an enviable approach—as simple and effective as her products.

Genesis® bakery systems. Paul Willett's entire business is about product development. His 15-point 'torture test' which each new product concept must survive is an excellent guide for any product developer. One of these points is that the new product must be patentable. According to Paul, the cost of patenting is simply one of the necessities of inventing. His patent, design and trademark registration costs run into the tens of thousands.

Registered designs and registrable design material

Registered designs are perhaps the most controversial form of intellectual property protection in Australia. This is possibly because they are often used incorrectly, with first-time product developers finding themselves without the protection they thought they had. However, the list of companies that use design registrations reads like a who's who of Australia's most recognised names and famous multinationals. Obviously design registrations have benefits to them.

To get the most out of your design registrations, it is important not to file for the one design you feel to be most appealing and commercially viable, due to the very specific protection dictated by a design registration. Design registrations are cheap, and often relatively straightforward to self-file, so it is worth filing for as many potential designs as you can.

The facts

A registered design is a formal nationwide monopoly granted by IP Australia. There are similar versions overseas: for instance, in the USA the equivalent form of protection is called a design patent. Registered designs protect the 'look' of an article rather than its function. Registered designs protect the features of 'pattern and ornamentation' and/or 'shape and configuration' applied to an article. Total protection lasts for 16 years. A registered trademark can be granted for certain aspects of packaging; this is preferable, as it gives indefinite protection.

Copyright is retained when a 2D design is applied to a 3D product (i.e. when a floral pattern is applied to a mug). However, copyright is almost always lost for mass-produced 3D items, such as fridge magnets. This grey area means that it is best to apply for design registration for any product destined for mass production.

Contact the state office of IP Australia and have staff send you a design registration kit, which outlines eligibility issues and application and filing fees. The kit also outlines special timing details that apply to registering designs in other countries. Again, design registration fees vary depending on the number of classes you choose for protection, on whether or not you use a patent attorney, and on whether you file overseas.

Make sure to alert your competitors to your protection by using the terms 'Design Registered', 'Design Protected', or actual design registration numbers on your product, packaging and promotional materials.

How the inventors in this book did it

Ztagg® surfing eyewear. Because of Robert Webster's experience with developing innovative surfboards in the past, he knew that he could affect his eligibility for patent and design registration protection if his invention became publicly known. He thus trialled his new eyewear concept on the back beaches. Along with a provisional patent application, Robert made applications for design registration of both the strap and the overall look of the sunglasses. Webster's patent attorney manages the entire patent and design registration process.

TROUBLE IN PARADISE SOLVED

It is hard to imagine that surfers suffer from anything, when they spend hours doing what they love most. But the fact is every surfer around the world is affected by severe glare caused by the sun reflecting off sand, the water, and especially off the white foam in the 'break zone'. This can lead to severe eye damage, skin cancer on the eyes' surface and on the sensitive skin around the eyes.

Robert Webster, devoted Gold Coast surfer for over 20 years and inventor of an exciting solution to this problem, says:

> The glare is so bright that it can actually be painful to open your eyes. There have been times when my mates and I have actually been temporarily blinded. The crazy thing is that every time I would get out on the water I would be reminded of this problem. But really this has existed for as long as people have been surfing, yet no-one, not even the massive, multi-national sunglass companies, has tackled this.

One day in 1994, as he and a group of friends were walking along the beach looking for a spot to set down their gear, they began talking about how they religiously wear sunglasses on the beach but take them off when they hit the water. According to Webster, this can actually compound the problem because the eyes are relaxed through the protection sunglasses offer, and then are dramatically affected when sunglasses are taken off and the eyes are hit with sudden glare:

> Walking back to my car that day after surfing for a few hours and trying to cope with glare again, it struck me that there has got to be an answer for this. There has to be some way to solve probably the main thing which can make surfing a hassle.

He and an employee from his surfboard manufacturing business began by identifying the main parameters for a successful eyewear solution and trying, as Webster calls it, 'to do a mind shift so that we would be open to radically different ideas':

> The basic issue is getting something to stay on your head and not get mangled when you're dumped by tons of water. After that, the eyewear can't fog up. It needs to give you total peripheral vision. It should be comfortable. And because there is a certain 'surfie style', it needs to look good too.

After months of R&D, they arrived at what Webster calls a two-tier approach:

> The sunglasses are based on the popular blade style with extra lens length for peripheral vision. We have also added a strap with a snap-release buckle to keep them in place, plus a rubber flange which provides grip and hold across the eye area and nose bridge. The second tier is achieved with a collar which goes around the back of the neck and has two stable strips which attach on either side of the sunglasses.

Though it sounds far out, the combination proved very successful when trialled by Webster and his employee. After he had made formal applications for a provisional patent and design registration, it was trialled with other surfers. Their feedback was consistently excellent.

But Webster laughs when he remembers how he and his employee trialled the new concept 'on the back beaches' to keep it under wraps:

> Because of my experience with innovative surfboard manufacturing, I knew that I could affect my eligibility for patent and design registration protection if my invention became publicly known. Once I was ready, I chose to initiate protection with a provisional patent application with IP Australia to gain a bit more R&D time, but to still be able to refer to my *priority date*. I also added design registration applications with IP Australia for both the strap and the overall look of the sunglasses.

During the provisional patent application period of 12 months, Webster felt ready to apply for patent protection in other countries. He did this through a PCT (Patent Cooperation Treaty) application and basically nominated the main surfing countries in which he aims to market his product. When this mass application period ends he enters the *national* phase, when you must make separate applications in each country and pay their fees and negotiate each different intellectual property system.

Webster's patent attorney, also a keen surfer, is instrumental in managing the entire domestic and overseas patent and design registration process. International intellectual property efforts can become complex and are certainly labour-intensive, when really, as Webster puts it, 'you just want to be out surfing'.

The product's name, 'Ztagg', is also the subject of applications to IP Australia for trademark registration, which will give Webster a nationwide monopoly in the several trademark classes he has chosen to protect the name in, such as class 9, which includes eyewear, and class 25, for clothing, footwear and headgear.

Although his R&D and intellectual property expenses are currently exceeding sales, Webster feels his concept is close to becoming a commercially viable product. But there is still hard work ahead. Says Webster:

> We now have to start educating surfers to wear this protective eyewear. But the Australian Surf Lifesaving Foundation has endorsed Ztagg™ and will begin marketing them. We are also attending the annual surf products trade show in San Diego, held every September. This will give us momentum into the American and European summer and hopefully this combined push will help establish this product strongly.

Expanda-Stand® brochure holders. Peter Eaton uses a powerful combination of a patent with design registrations. This way he protects not only the unique way his product functions but also the essential design elements. This method of protecting form and function is used by many top product developers.

GroGuard® wine vine trainers. Unfortunately for Graham Due and his business partner, inadequate design protection led to a competitor springing up overnight and taking advantage of the product in which Due had invested months of hard work and thousands of dollars in R&D. After completing the product's R&D phase, Due set out to protect his product by applying for a design registration. The application cost $90 at the time, and the subsequent registration fee for the first year's protection was under $200. 'Small bikkies when you consider how much money we had already committed to the product', said Due. However, one design registration wasn't enough: 'If you want watertight protection, you should protect as many potential versions as possible, along with the one that you see as the most marketable. This way you don't give an opportunistic competitor any room to manoeuvre.'

INTELLECTUAL PROPERTY PROTECTION IN THE REAL WORLD

There is nothing quite like turning on the television for a bit of light entertainment and seeing that your new product has been shortlisted for a popular national business award. But, as if somehow caught in an alternative universe where things are not what they seem to be, the product is in fact a knock-off of your product, and the business in the running to win thousands of dollars is not yours.

According to Graham Due, inventor of an innovative vine guard that protects and 'trains' young grape vines, this alternative universe quickly became a nightmare. 'My business partner and I had our solicitor contact the award organisers, but we were never sure if this competitor was taken off the shortlist or not', says Due from his Adelaide premises:

> The day the award was to be announced, I just wasn't game to turn on the TV. My partner rang me to say they hadn't won, and we breathed a sigh of relief. But, really, the damage to our business and our market had already been done.

Looking back, Due and his partner believe that a lack of knowledge about protecting their intellectual property and how to combat infringement had contributed to the worst-case scenario they now confronted. For stronger protection, you should protect as many potential versions as possible, along with the one that you see as the most marketable. It is also important to make applications to IP Australia immediately after R&D is completed, but well before the design is prepared for commercial production. According to Gary Kichenside of IP Australia, 'If you release your design to the public or to potential buyers, say through a trade show or catalogue before you apply, you will have made the one common but deadly mistake which quite simply blows your eligibility for design registration out of the water'.

Not content to play second fiddle to their new competition, Due and his partner have turned a negative into a positive: Gro-Guard® is competing strongly both on quality and price, and is available in many of the finest vineyards across Australia and in important overseas markets, such as the USA. There are other related products slated for imminent release. Says Due:

> Our approach to intellectual property protection is considerably more savvy now than when we first started out. Our only consolation is that intellectual property information has really been thin on the ground, and I know that other product-oriented businesses like ours have experienced a few of the classic intellectual property pitfalls. But one thing we do consistently, and actually did from the start, is apply for trademark registration so that we have a monopoly over that name in the goods classes we choose.

Two new products to be launched simultaneously here and initially in the USA, ZipSafe® and ZipSure®, are the subject of patent applications in Australia and overseas as well as international trademark registrations. Due and his partner are continuing to invest in R&D, improved production methods, as well as seeking out innovative marketing techniques. Says Due:

> I don't think there is a business on this planet that wants competition, and certainly we could have done without the headaches of a competitor when we were only getting on our feet. But the reality is that competition makes you hungrier. It forces you to work smarter and not rest on your laurels. What we have found about intellectual property protection is that uninformed decisions can be worse than not protecting at all because you are lulled into a false sense of protection, whereas correct protection choices are definitely worth the expense of application and registration fees.

Plant breeders' rights and registrable material

Plant breeders' rights are obtained from Plant Breeders Rights Australia. Much like a patent, they protect and provide exclusive commercial rights for a new plant variety. You must be able to prove that the variety is distinct, as well as uniform and stable. Rights last up to 25 years for trees and vines, and 20 years for other species. Call Plant Breeders Rights Australia for your free information and application kit (see Appendix).

Copyright

Copyright is automatic protection for literary and artistic works. It also protects original technical drawings, renderings, training manuals, software programs, product concepts, promotional materials (brochures, posters, films and videos) and other similar materials. Protection generally lasts 50 years from the year of the author's death or from the year of first publication, depending on the material. Copyright for films, broadcasts and sound recordings lasts 50 years from their making. Get yourself into the habit of always adding the copyright line to anything for which you own copyright. This includes:

- representations of your product idea, such as proto-types, renderings, photographs, videos, animations and written descriptions;
- promotional materials, such as your presentation package, brochures, fact sheets, press releases and videos;
- other materials, such as instruction sheets, product manuals and packaging.

Sample copyright line:
© Year Your Name or Business Name. All rights reserved.

How the inventors in this book did it

- My Place® mini business package—This information package based on the three-in-one baby product I invented is essentially a paper-based kit. I have inserted a copyright line on each and every page, as well as on the actual product's pattern.

- All the inventors in this book have created promotional materials at one time or another. Each is automatically copyright-protected whether a copyright line is applied or not. However, it is advisable that you always provide this line as a deterrent to would-be competitors. In fact, in some countries, not providing the copyright line on items you consider to be protected could mean that you will fail to receive the full remuneration amount if you need to go to court and the case is awarded in your favour.

- Almost all the inventors in this book would have created drawings, drafts, prototypes, taken photographs and so on. All of these items are automatically copyright-protected.

Circuit layout rights

Circuit layout rights automatically protect original layout designs for integrated circuits, computer chips etc. The maximum protection period is 20 years. Accordingly, rights to an original layout subsist for 10 years from first commercial exploitation (within the first 10 years of creation, and 10 years from the year in which it was made, if not commercially exploited).

Trade secrets

The beauty of the trade secret is that you never divulge details of your invention to the public, as you do with patents. It is often used to protect manufacturing processes and knowhow. But it is protective only when the manufacturing process or knowhow cannot be reverse-engineered and is kept tightly under wraps. A trade secret is an intellectual property right you can automatically assign to yourself. You do not and cannot apply for protection to any authority. One helpful way of determining whether or not to use a trade secret as protection is to conduct an infringement test (see the next section for more detail).

To establish and maintain the integrity of a trade secret, you must rely on legal contracts drafted by your commercial solicitor for anyone who comes into contact with this information. If you have employees and/or subcontractors, have them sign a legal agreement that keeps them from divulging confidential information or benefiting from this information during or after their employment with you. You must also scrupulously use confidentiality agreements for any external party with whom you share trade secrets—say, to initiate a potential commercial association.

How the inventors in this book did it

Living Picture® process. Michael Beverley's process could easily have been patented. However, as this valuable process is used in manufacturing and it would be difficult for his competitors to reverse-engineer his results, he wisely chose to keep it a trade secret. Patenting his process would involve revealing the details of his process, making him vulnerable to competition, of which there is currently none in the southern hemisphere. However, Michael did choose to gain a registered trademark as the marketing 'front' for his process.

THE MAIN MUG

You couldn't find a more apt trademark than Living Picture® for Michael Beverley's innovative mug-decoration process. What makes these mugs stand out from the crowd is the sheer brillance and clarity of their imagery. Also remarkable is that the imagery covers over 90% of the mug, from top to bottom and side to side. The mugs are alive with colour. The shelves of Michael's Gold Coast showroom are a jumble of dozens of mugs, each covered in famous imagery, from well-known corporate IDs to Elvis.

'This is the most expensive mug in the southern hemisphere', says Michael, holding up a mug featuring an action shot from Star Wars®. 'It sells for about $12 retail, but in my eyes it's the culmination of thousands of dollars in R&D and about two and a half years of blood, sweat and tears.'

If you think the coffee mug is a fairly obscure product to focus your energies on, think again. Coffee mugs are one of the most popular gift items around the world, especially when emblazoned with the latest in movies, famous personalities, cartoon characters, prime-time TV programs, and other hot imagery. Sales worldwide go into many millions.

Though Michael now owns and runs The Mug Factory®, devoted to his process and providing specially coated mugs to the domestic photo mug trade, this wasn't always the case. Michael was working in sales and moonlighting as a freelance computer technician when, on a trip to the USA, he noticed some very different mugs. He says:

> When I returned to Australia I identified that this kind of dynamic mug was not available on the market. I really wanted to see if I could figure out how they were made and maybe go a step further. I began developing a process involving the application of specially printed papers to specially coated mugs with heat and pressure.

The results were usually frustratingly close, but not of the quality he was striving for. 'I basically had to endlessly test different inks, different papers and different heat and pressure settings. It was always three steps forward and four steps back, but eventually I cracked it', he adds.

What he had 'cracked' was a process known to only two other companies in the world, and none in the southern hemisphere. Not only does it result in eye-catching and appealing mugs but the process is considerably cheaper and less labour-intensive than traditional decoration processes.

'The key to a mug's success', says Michael, 'is not what the consumer is going to put inside it, but what the consumer sees on the outside when it's sitting on the shop shelf. Like a lot of very popular gift products these days, coffee mugs are really just extremely successful vehicles for licensed imagery.' Known as licensed properties, this imagery is bought for a set time and price from the licence-holders, such as Warner Bros, Walt Disney & Company, and Gaffney International. Michael says:

> This is a multi-million-dollar industry for the simple reason that people all over the world will often choose a product decorated with licensed imagery instead of one without it. As long as it's popular, the imagery could just as easily come direct from Hollywood, like Star Wars, or originate from Australia, like Bananas in Pyjamas.

Because Michael was not a licensee of these images and licences run in the hundreds of thousands of dollars, he approached one of Australia's largest giftware manufacturers, which now licenses the process and pays Michael a per-mug royalty. He says:

> Thankfully I knew enough about patenting to know that it would be best for my process to remain a trade secret. To market the process, though, I immediately sought registration for the Living Picture trademark. Even though I didn't know much about inventing and intellectual property principles, I am glad I knew this much.

> In the beginning, Michael financed his R&D through his two jobs and a small family loan. 'Luckily I was a bachelor, because you couldn't have fed more than one person on what I was living on', Michael laughs and waves his arms towards the shelves of brilliant mugs, 'but, as you can see, it was all worth it'.

Nad's® hair-removal gel. Sue Ismiel could also have gained a patent for her process, but chose not to reveal her vital ingredients to potential competitors. Like Michael, she chose a registered trademark to strengthen her product's position in the marketplace.

Confidential information

Confidential information is essentially all of the other information that should remain secret, such as your R&D results, technical details, financial plans, customer databases—anything you would not want in the hands of a competitor. Although confidential information is not strictly intellectual property, it often supports intellectual property and general business efforts, and so is highly valuable. Like trade secrets, confidential information can remain protected through legal agreements if it needs to be shared with other parties.

What is an infringement test?

Infringement, in the jargon, means your product is copied by an unauthorised party. An infringement test is one way of determining whether to patent or maintain a trade secret. It is primarily used for manufacturing processes and formulas, where it may be harder or even impossible to tell whether intellectual property has been infringed. If it is impossible to tell whether your process or formula has been infringed, then an expensive patent may not be a good use of your protection dollar. A trade secret would probably suffice.

To work out your own infringement test, determine how you would know that your intellectual property had been infringed. One inventor of a special dishwasher-safe coating for ceramics regularly buys his competitor's product and subjects it to rigorous testing. So far, the competing product has not shown signs of his unique coating. The day it does, he will know either that he has been infringed or that his competitor has managed to develop their own coating. He has another strategy in place in case this happens.

Obviously you will know when your trademark has been infringed when you find it being used by someone else. One of the best ways to keep on top of this is to conduct regular searches of both the *Yellow Pages* and Australian Securities Commission home pages on the Internet. Both are free and you can search any name you choose. I am aware of one Queensland inventor who did a casual search of the *Yellow Pages* and found several businesses around the country using his registered trademark and trading in an area that would clearly infringe his registered trademark.

Infringement action

Once you have found out that your intellectual property has been infringed, what will you do? Your options relate to what right has been infringed—formal or automatic—and how much money you are willing to devote to fighting the breach. Speak to your commercial solicitor immediately. Your first option, and, if you are lucky, the only one you will need, is a forceful letter demanding that the infringing party cease and desist from trading with the breached intellectual property.

One of the bitter realities of inventing is that, if your rights are infringed, you may not have the money to pursue a court action. According to many of the inventors featured in this book, they would rather spend tens of thousands of dollars on improving their product than on defending their patent.

If you are involved in a commercial relationship with another party, such as an investor, business angel or through a licensing agreement, then it needs to be stipulated who is responsible for attacking infringement and how this action will be paid for.

Occasionally, infringement is unintentional. This can result in some strange bedfellows, who both benefit from the forced association. A famous range of Australian children's imagery was accidentally infringed by a well-known Australian sock manufacturer. The sock people did the right thing and approached the licensor of the children's imagery with a sock they had gone into production with. They decided to do a deal and everyone was happy.

Secrets to saving thousands when protecting your product idea

Perhaps the biggest obstacle to successfully getting product ideas on the market is running out of money because of hefty protection costs. Patent, design and trademark costs snowball as your applications proceed through various stages. These expenses usually mount up at a time when you are far from receiving any return on your financial outlay. The following are ways in which you can reduce your protection expenses and pace the spending of your funds.

Don't protect your idea in its earliest form. Make sure your R&D has been completed so that the protection you seek is for your product idea's most final form and you are not forced to reapply after each major refinement.

Self-file your applications when you can, especially for straightforward Australian trademark and design applications. You will find IP Australia's official application forms are not too challenging and you will feel more confident after completing each one. Official fees are low. Don't be afraid to ask questions of IP Australia staff and get them to help you understand application questions and how your application will proceed through the system.

Shop around and find out what patent and trademark attorney services cost. Before you sit down with a patent or trademark attorney, know how much the official patent, trademark and design registration fees are. Then compare them with what the patent attorney charges. (This is much like the gap between Medicare and what your doctor charges.) Knowing this will help you shop around between the various firms. Ask each for a schedule of how and when their fees will apply. This is not common and you may be put off, but insist. Most inventors tell me they wish they had initially understood how much they would end up paying and how often they would receive bills.

Know your intellectual property rights. Take the time to completely understand each intellectual property right so that you can make sensible decisions about which to use.

Don't beat a dead horse. Know when to back off from seeking further protection, or from advancing to different stages of the protection system, when the signs are clear that your product is unlikely to progress to commercialisation.

When filing overseas, get your priorities straight. When you decide to file for protection overseas, make sure you choose those countries that are your most important markets, and/or where you want to or could probably manufacture your product. Protecting in major manufacturing markets should inhibit people in these countries from producing your product and exporting it to markets you are not protected in.

If you use each of these recommendations, you will save thousands of dollars in protecting your product idea. As well, you will have a clear picture of your protection expenses and of when you will need to pay both official and patent attorney fees. This information is critical to determining exactly how much money, finance or investment you will need to see you through commercialisation and beyond.

How best to use the services of patent and trademark attorneys

Patent and trademark attorneys are specialists in the protection of intellectual property. Traditionally they specialise in preparing and filing applications for patents, trademarks and designs with IP Australia and overseas intellectual property offices. Some offer other related services, such as intellectual property audits and licensing agreements. A patent or trademark attorney will act as your representative throughout the process of gaining protection through IP Australia. He or she will provide counterarguments when an IP Australia examiner finds some barrier to your application, which is common. As such, a competent attorney can often make the difference between getting a patent, trademark or design under contentious circumstances, such as when your invention/innovation breaks new ground and creates a precedent in eligibility for protection.

Your local Australian patent and trademark attorney must act on your behalf when seeking protection overseas, as foreign IP offices require a local 'address for service' and will not deal direct with non-citizens. Therefore, Australian attorneys have links with attorneys in other countries. They arrange translation of application documents and generally smooth your way through foreign intellectual property systems.

I have heard stories of disgust with *and* adoration of patent and trademark attorneys. While most are reputable and helpful, as with any group of professionals some are not. Peter Fisher, patent attorney and senior partner in the Brisbane firm Fisher Adams and Kelly, feels that those patent and trademark attorneys that 'get it right' view education and a close and honest working relationship as integral to their role:

> Once an inventor has their Eureka! moment, they are thrust into a whole new world and this can be confusing and pretty dazzling. There is an enormous amount of complex detail to come to grips with, so initially my role is to help my client understand what they're in for. Then one of our main aims is to help our client see past their initial solution to one specific problem. But to do this, the inventor needs to relax. I can't tell you how many times an inventor has walked in with a mysterious paper bag, which unfortunately remains a mystery throughout our entire meeting. To really give first-class service, we need to be a part of the evolution of their idea. There needs to be give and take—a two-way street—which leads to a close working relationship.

Where patent and trademark attorneys have gone wrong probably fits into the 'shonk' and 'pipedreams' categories. Inventors have spoken of being guaranteed commercial success, and then being rushed into major commitments from their first meeting, only to find their product idea over- or under-protected at a later date. The inventor is also overwhelmed by the continuing stream of hefty and confusing bills. Unfortunately, bad patent attorneys are relying on first-time inventors who have not educated themselves in any area of inventing and commercialisation.

The following are some tips for dealing with patent and trademark attorneys effectively.

- Shop around. Get referrals from other inventors through your local inventors' club or industry networks. The large firms tend to get most of their work from big business, including overseas companies. They often have a stable of patent and trademark attorneys with very specialist knowledge, ranging from electronic engineering to chemical formulas. The smaller, boutique firms tend to have more competitive rates and can be less daunting. Both have their merits and each firm, no matter what size, will have its own culture. Be open to referrals and feel free to have an initial discussion with a handful of attorneys (the first visit is usually free) until you find the one you feel most comfortable with and who will offer you value for money. Remember, you're paying the bill.

- You can meet a patent or trademark attorney fairly early on if you want, but do not file any applications until you have taken your product idea through R&D.

- Before you meet, make sure you get enough information about patenting and registered trademarks and designs that you are an informed participant in the protection process.

- Patent and trademark attorneys have their own schedule of fees above and beyond the official IP Australia fees, as well as fees for handling examiner and other queries. Ask for a schedule of fees at your first visit so that you can anticipate and budget for expenses.

- You will be inundated by paper and a variety of bills. Start a file now so that each can be referred to later.

- Patent and trademark attorneys are generally not solicitors. In fact, even solicitors who are specialists in intellectual property cannot make applications on your behalf unless they are also patent or trademark attorneys.

- Patent attorneys are vital to preparing patent documents and negotiating the system for you. However, you may want to self-file Australian trademark and design registration applications if these are relatively straightforward. You will save money, but you will need to keep track of your application as it makes its way through the system and to note all upcoming anniversary dates.

- If you receive a bill from a patent or trademark attorney that you don't understand, query it. You may end up doing a lot of this, as patent attorney bills are notoriously difficult to understand.

- Do not ask the patent attorney whether he/she is interested in a share of your potential profits in lieu of payment. A reputable patent attorney will patiently tell you what he/she has probably told dozens, if not hundreds of inventors: 'I need to remain objective.'

- If you decide not to proceed with further protection action, notify your patent or trademark attorney in writing. If your patent attorney rings you and asks whether you want to proceed and you are willing to do so, ask him/her to fax you the question, note your verbal response and file it. Or, better yet, reply in writing.

- Do not be afraid to sack your patent or trademark attorney (which I have done in the past), but do it swiftly and in writing. Make sure you require that the attorney transfer all of your files to your address or to that of your new firm.

The intellectual property portfolio

You would expect medium to large Australian businesses to have a firm grip on their intellectual property, considering they have the money to throw at this priority matter. But through my seminar series on intellectual property strategy, aimed primarily at managing directors and CEOs, I am consistently surprised that most have no idea exactly how many intellectual property assets they have, or how these are protected.

Of course, small business people, who are by and large struggling to keep their heads above water, almost never consider their intellectual property assets, even though these are often the foundation of the entire business. Yet this is a powerful portfolio, which can be compiled through a simple inventory or audit. Solo inventors and product developers often assume that they have only one bit of intellectual property (i.e. their great idea). In reality, the average inventor can have several assets, for example:

1. main invention or product idea—patent/design registration;
2. product's design features—design registration;
3. product's name—trademark registration;
4. product's promotional materials—copyright;
5. R&D behind the product—confidential information;
6. manufacturing process—patent/trade secret;
7. technical details and drawings—confidential information/ copyright;

8. customer list—confidential information;
9. financial details and plans—confidential information;
10. information/presentation package—copyright/confidential information.

When you create your own intellectual property portfolio, which you can do with a simple spreadsheet or database program, or even a piece of paper in landscape format, make sure you include at least the following column categories:

- the intellectual property asset (i.e. product name, invention);
- the protection each asset has (i.e. registered trademark, registered design, patent);
- in which countries the asset is protected (e.g. Australia and the USA);
- when the protection began (e.g. 1999);
- when it will end (e.g. 2029);
- any vital anniversary dates for paying fees (e.g. annually in June).

This comprehensive, factual portfolio will be very appealing to any bank manager, potential investor or licensee. Just as importantly, it will make it clear to you just how many valuable assets you have.

Legal contracts and the commercialisation process

There are a number of legal contracts that help to support your intellectual property rights. They will usually be drafted by a commercial solicitor in consultation with you. Some of these contracts may even be available in standard form for a set fee, as opposed to an hourly rate. Your local inventors' association could be a useful source for a referral and possibly even for standard forms.

Confidentiality agreements/non-disclosure forms

A confidentiality agreement may also be referred to as a non-disclosure form. These are available as a standard form from most solicitors and inventors' associations. A confidentiality agreement is a relatively brief legal document (from one to several pages long), and lays out the terms by which you are sharing information about your invention/ product idea with another party. It is a good starting point for a mutually beneficial commercial association.

Once a confidentiality agreement has been signed by both parties, its aim is to allow you to share vital details without the other party being able to steal these ideas. Sometimes a party will not sign a confidentiality agreement because they are working on a similar invention or in a related area. Make sure you also use your confidentiality agreement when you seek help from service-providers, such as graphic designers or prototypers, to help you transform your idea into a tangible form.

Confidentiality agreements are not usually necessary when dealing with professional advisers, as they are bound by professional codes of ethics preventing them from pursuing your idea themselves or revealing it to others without your permission.

Employee/subcontractor agreements

Employee/subcontractor agreements can be complex documents covering a variety of employment issues, and including a clause about confidentiality. Or they can be solely about confidentiality. Essentially, these agreements mean that an employee/subcontractor cannot take specific information or knowledge gained while in your employ to another employer or use it in their own enterprise. The agreement cannot include aspects of their employment that are universal to that trade or profession.

Deeds of assignment

A deed of assignment is a contract used between you and an external service-provider, such as a prototyper or graphic designer, to ensure that the intellectual property created while working for you is formally transferred to you. It would be prepared by a commercial solicitor and is not a complex or lengthy document.

Though there is an unspoken agreement that any work commissioned by you is your intellectual property, it is best not to take this for granted. Some service-providers traditionally retain copyright: photographers, for example, almost always claim copyright of their photo of your product idea, unless otherwise negotiated and a deed of assignment is signed. I am aware of at least one case of a graphic designer successfully arguing that the copyright to a logo was effectively his as the bill had not been paid, so assignment had not occurred. Because of the potential grey area, this particular form of contract is gaining popularity.

Licensing agreements

A licensing agreement is a formal contract between you and the business that has agreed to license your product idea. (See Chapter 5 on licensing your product idea for a comprehensive definition, as well as the elements of a successful agreement.)

Heads of agreement

A heads of agreement can initiate, or be the precursor to, a formal licence agreement. It is a more informal and shortened version which roughly outlines the main points of agreement between two parties. This should evolve fairly quickly into a complete licensing agreement. It cannot be relied on as a final contract because it is not detailed enough to deal with any difficulties that might arise.

4 Get More Money to Commercialise Your Idea

When to seek more money

The inventor's perennial problem is money—or, more accurately, the lack of it. Experts in finance and investment will tell you not to seek bank loans or investment until you have completed research and development, your idea is protected or official applications have been filed, and it is in some tangible form that makes it easy to be considered and understood. Also, before your idea is better tested and complete, asking for loans or investment from family and friends could expose them to unreasonable risk.

This means that you will have to rely on your own cash and/or credit to pay for at least the early stages of commercialisation (as outlined in Chapter 1), which can include quite a few bills for thousands of dollars each for prototyping, intellectual property protection and advisers' fees. However, if you pace and balance your spending against the reality of your R&D, your financial investment can be kept within reasonable bounds. Your willingness to sink your own funds into your product concept is also an important indicator that you are willing to take a risk with something you are expecting others to take a punt on.

Preparing to seek finance and/or investment

Once you have made it past the self-funded stages of commercialisation and are keen to bring in money from other sources, you will want to make sure you are properly prepared. A sharp accountant and realistic business plan are vital. Start by being very clear about how much money you need.

According to Zeke Ezra, partner with Duesburys Chartered Accountants and someone who has raised millions in investment dollars for sole inventors:

> Most inventors are afraid to be up-front about exactly how much they need for fear of being laughed out of the room. The problem with not asking for the correct amount is that you end up on a financial dripfeed. You get what you need for one stage, and then to proceed it becomes critical to ask for more funds. Not only does the venture suffer from the lack of appropriate finance, most investors and bank managers will bail out at this point.

I have myself experienced this 'dripfeed' syndrome. I started my commercialisation efforts with my own income, then needing more cash I sold shares in my company to close family and friends. When I decided to buy stock from my overseas licensee I gained a bank loan, and when these goods proved faulty I ended up with an overdraft. The net result was significant debt. And although it's fair to say that I struck some bad luck, in the form of faulty goods and a dishonest overseas licensee, small, badly timed injections of money contributed to the ultimate failure of my initial commercialisation efforts.

The alternative to establishing an overall amount required for successful commercialisation, which I later used very successfully for the very same product, is to work within a set budget and allow each progression to pay for itself— much like the ripple effect you get when you throw a stone into a pond. Sue Ismiel started with $5000 to buy the ingredients and packaging for a limited amount of her hair-removal gel. She used the profits from the sale of these units to progress to the next level of business. Peter Thorne has combined this approach with a small loan from his bank.

Investment and finance also involves significant and complex taxation issues. 'If you don't sort out your taxation position early on, it will cost you later in both time and money. Commercialisation is hard enough without also having to deal with taxation penalties', says Zeke Ezra. It is a rare inventor who also has an accountancy background. Most, including myself, find they are totally out of their depth when it comes to taxation and other end-of-financial-year issues. This is why I cannot overstate the need to surround yourself with competent advisers, especially those who have direct experience with new product com-mercialisation.

You will need to seek your accountant's advice about which business structure to establish, such as a registered business or company. Also very important is who owns your intellectual property if you decide to establish a business or company. It is almost always preferable for you to personally own all intellectual property assets and license them through a formal agreement for a nominal fee to your business or company. These assets are then protected should your enterprise fail, and they can be inherited by your children or sold as personal assets to other parties.

Other than the numbers, your success in gaining the

funds you need can be greatly influenced by a combination of factors outside your product concept. How compelling these factors are determine what Zeke refers to as your 'position of strength', which he outlines as follows:

- a sound and detailed business plan;
- your expertise (though not necessarily with this product);
- a track record (which need not have been with this product or even involving product commercialisation);
- a commercially viable product which can easily be demonstrated and understood;
- market research, usually of a professional calibre;
- intellectual property protection, especially patents or at least applications, in suitable countries;
- a willingness to invest in the product yourself.

The stronger each element is, the more you can shop around to get the right loan, the right partner or the right investor. It is true that 1% of something is better than 100% of nothing, but you do need to remain in control.

This means not seeking or accepting a loan you cannot possibly service, or committing yourself to a partner or investor you don't think you can work with for valid reasons (many inventors are so married to their idea they reject sound advice and are impossible to work with). Finding appropriate finance and/or investment takes time. Do not be surprised if, just when you think the money is in the bank or the cheque's in the mail, it all unravels and you have to start again. This is a common thread throughout commercialisation, and if you are following your goals sensibly setbacks will not be tragedies—they will just be setbacks.

How and where to seek more money

There are a variety of ways to raise cash, based on how much you are looking for and what kind of arrangement suits you. Essentially there are four major ways to raise cash: debt, equity, government assistance, and self-funding.

Debt-based finance

With this option you will maintain full control of your project and all profits, but will take on some form of debt and generally high interest rates. Your main options are:

- loans—for most sole inventors, these will be personal loans from an institutional lender or finance agency, or from family and friends;
- credit cards, or a rise in your credit limit;
- overdrafts/lines of credit.

Because you are unlikely to gain debt-based finance based on your product idea (except from family and friends), you will need to meet the general criteria for personal loan eligibility. Nevertheless, have your presentation package ready for your loan interview.

Institutional lenders

Inventors have patchy luck with most institutional lenders, such as banks, credit unions and finance agencies. I have spoken to many who could not get a cent from them. Then there are others who have managed to gain loans and overdrafts.

This is not a good option if you need more than $10 000.

> ### Criteria for success
>
> - Your presentation package should include a business plan or some level of supporting material for the amount of money you are asking for.

- Your ability to service the loan is paramount. This is more likely if you already have little or no debt, have a permanent income, or have established a track record of sales with your product.

- Most bank managers live and die by the numbers, so your supporting materials, such as research results and a business plan, could prove crucial.

- Some bank managers are swayed by the strength of the advisers you have around you and their opinions of your potential for success.

- An existing relationship and track record with the particular institution you are seeking money from helps.

- Being clear and confident about a specific amount and how that money is to be used will have influence. This is especially true when funds will be used to create assets such as formally granted intellectual property protection, like patents.

Equity

Business angels

Business angels are investors who not only provide financial input but bring their own knowledge, experience and skills to the arrangement, very often in a mentor-type role. They become active participants either in all areas of commercialisation activity or only in that area in which they have specific expertise.

There are a number of matching services available in Australia to bring inventors and investors together. Usually the matching process is done by either the inventor or the investor, such as with a service called 'Ideas and the investor' (see Appendix). Occasionally, the matching service is aided by a person who is familiar with the individuals in their database, much like the traditional matchmaker. Chris Kaine's Business Angels, based in Melbourne, is a service based on this model (see Appendix).

There are matching services featured on the Net and in several business magazines. There are also books dedicated to this subject.

This is a good option if you need less than $100 000 and more than just financial assistance.

Criteria for success

- Your presentation package should include a concise summary of your business plan.

- You should be able to present your plan dynamically and demonstrate your product.

- Many successful matches have been made, but because there is more than money involved these matches must involve a high level of personal compatibility to be fully successful.

- A legal contract is essential.

Business partners

Business partners are one of the most controversial forms of financial assistance. This is because a business partner is often a friend or family member, or someone introduced to the inventor by either a friend or family member. When the partnerships fail, as they tend to do, they fail on a personal as well as a business level. Many of these failed partnerships can take years to recover from, as John Sinclair will attest. But others inventors, like Max Moorhouse, have found this kind of arrangement perfect for their needs. The message is to be wary, and remember that most friendships do not survive the strain of the commercialisation process— especially when the partner brings cash and no skills, and so is unable to take part in the day-to-day activity.

Most business partners bring less than $100 000 to the table.

Criteria for success

- Your presentation package should include a concise summary of your business plan.

- You should be able to present your plan dynamically and demonstrate your product.

- A high level of personal compatibility is needed.

- A legal contract is essential.

Venture capital

Venture capital is money invested by an individual or firm in a new venture or enterprise. It is often associated with high-risk activities, so the return is usually expected to be high as well. Venture capitalists are seasoned players who are looking for highly profitable enterprises with the potential for explosive growth. They tend to target high-tech businesses and those with the potential to go public. They often invest a combination of their own money and that of other wealthy individuals.

There are numerous venture capital opportunities available on the Net and often advertised in business magazines. Your accountant may also be a source of investors willing to provide venture capital.

This is a good option if you need significantly more than $100 000.

Criteria for success

- Your presentation package absolutely must include:
  — a comprehensive, very detailed business plan (and financial statements if you have them);
  — background details of yourself and of any others who are a part of your commercialisation efforts;
  — professional, current market research.

- You should be able to present your plan dynamically and demonstrate your product.

- A legal contract will be required.

Seed capital

Seed capital is funds provided at the R&D stage. Because these funds are provided at such a risky point in the commercialisation process, seed capital is rare and usually given only to inventors with a previously successful track record.

Government assistance

Government assistance for sole inventors is rare. Most government assistance is aimed at established small to medium business operators. However, there are the New Enterprise Incentive Scheme and AusIndustry to consider.

Many in the inventing game will tell you to forget government assistance and get on with the hard work of finding privately available finance or investment. It is true that many inventors have felt the government 'owed' them something. This attitude, and their wait for help that never eventuates, usually paralyses all progress. Other innovative small business people have been granted important sums of money to continue with R&D, to conduct important studies and so on. Willie Erken points to his AusIndustry grant as an important turning point in his commercialisation path. There are also consultants who specialise in gaining government assistance for their clients. Many do not charge unless they are successful. You may be able to gain a referral to such a consultant through an inventors' association or through another professional adviser.

Don't close any doors on yourself, but at the same time be willing to seek out other financial opportunities.

The New Enterprise Incentive Scheme

Other than being unemployed, you must have a viable new product or service idea to be eligible for the New Enterprise Incentive Scheme. Places are limited. The program includes business training and a small amount of seed capital to proceed with your idea. Individuals as well as groups can apply. You will be eligible for office space and business counselling through a business 'incubator' (essentially serviced offices with an in-house business counsellor), if there is one in your area. Contact the Department of Employment, Education and Training in your state or territory for more information.

This is a good option if you are willing to start up your enterprise on a shoestring, and perhaps seek more cash from other sources after you have established a track record.

Criteria for success

- Your presentation package is esssential.
- Request an application form to establish eligibility requirements.

AusIndustry

AusIndustry is the government's main port of call for innovators. It offers a range of services and financial assistance, although it is rare for this help to go to sole inventors. It is best to ring AusIndustry's national hotline and speak to an adviser (see Appendix).

Assistance can range from subsidised professional services to fairly significant loans and grants.

Criteria for success

■ Depending on the program or loan, your presentation package may be required.

■ Request an application form or speak to a hotline adviser to establish eligibility requirements.

Self-funding

With the self-funding approach, growth funds further growth. This is most appropriate at the cottage-industry level. The following are your options with self-funding, other than those already listed (e.g. credit cards and personal loans):

■ selling existing units of your product and using this cash to pay for each subsequent step in expansion;

■ pre-selling unmade units and using this cash to pay for production;

■ using prepaid orders, or a significant but as yet unpaid order with a large distributor, to gain 30-day terms with suppliers;

■ factoring receipts with a factoring agency, which will provide cash up front and take a percentage of your receipts;

■ using publicity to gain interest and sales;

■ taking on commission-only sales reps.

5 Licensing Versus Self-manufacturing Your Idea

Deciding which road to take

Many of the inventors featured in this book have decided to self-manufacture their idea. They have created an entire business enterprise from their efforts and, by and large, receive a greater return than they would from a licensing agreement. Most of these inventors are directly responsible for every aspect of their product's success—manufacturing, sales and distribution, marketing and public relations. All of the inventors in this group have retained consultant experts in various fields, some on a regular basis and others as needed.

Other inventors, such as Warren Wilson, have chosen to license their product idea and receive royalty payments, which is something that most inventors dream of doing. A licensing agreement, especially a lucrative one, can give you a financial return without the structure and complexity of a business.

However, according to Andrew Holt, former president of the Canberra Inventors' Association, it is advisable to take the longer road of self-manufacturing:

> If you can afford to wait, and surround yourself with the right people, self-manufacturing is much more profitable in the long run. As well, you can begin with self-manufacturing on a small, cottage-industry scale to prove your product's popularity and 'saleability'. Then, after you have developed a track record over a year or two, you will be in a significantly stronger position to license your product and walk away with royalties. Or perhaps even sell, or franchise the entire business.

Certainly this is the case for John Sinclair, who self-manufactures his gold medal-winning invention but is now negotiating licensing agreements with keen overseas interests. However, Sinclair is quick to point out that this combination has been possible only because the product is a proven one, and has won major international awards.

WHO SAID WINNING AN OSCAR IS ONLY FOR MOVIE STARS?

In 1979, when John Sinclair was only a young lad, he bought himself a flash new stereo system, only to find that he didn't have enough power outlets in his room to plug it in. To enjoy his new hifi, he had double adapters on top of double adapters, and electrical cords all over the place—an electrical nightmare by any standard.

That's when he had his Eureka! moment. He asked himself, 'What if you could plug an electrical appliance in anywhere you liked?'. He began making sketches of what was essentially a skirting board containing electrical cabling. 'Perhaps it was my youth, but I put the idea aside when a friend of mine said, "Who the hell is going to change their outlets just because you said so?"', says John. Around four years later, a close friend mentioned the electrical skirting board idea and convinced John it was just too good to gather dust. Thus began a nearly 20-year saga.

John took his drawings around to electricians, and their response and advice was extremely favourable. 'I decided to file a provisional patent specification. When I look back at that application now, I have to laugh. It was more my life's story than a summary of an invention', he says. In a strange twist, the rights to that patent were bought by an infamous Perth businessman who sat on it for two years. The patents actually lapsed during this time.

A few more years passed. Then John realised that if his idea was ever going to make it to the shop shelves he would have to design a system that complied with Australian Standards. He then linked up with his best mate of 20 years. 'That was my next mistake', says John. 'Never go into business with your best mate if you want to stay friends.' They filed for a new patent application. But their relationship deteriorated after the introduction of a third partner and a lack of product development. He is still fighting a court battle regarding this company and the high-profile interests who became involved.

But John learned that there were friends who still had his best interests at heart. A childhood friend who had watched the saga from afar suggested that John ring his sister, a practising accountant. Patricia Strick turned out to be a godsend, helping John sort out much of the mess of the past few years. Eventually, with the help of Sead Strick, Patricia's husband and a qualified builder knowledgeable about the building trade, they formed a company called Universal Power Track Pty Ltd.

According to John, together they have accomplished more in the past three years than in the past 17 years or so combined. 'Sure we have our moments. I think all partnerships do, but we listen to each other and always put the product and the company's interests first', says John. Slowly and carefully, they have built up the product and the business:

> I believe an inventor should learn how to crawl before he can walk, and walk before he can run. Do your research and save yourself a lot of mistakes. Believe in your product and listen to advice without jealousy, as this advice can very often lead you to an excellent solution to a problem.

The business now manufactures, sells and installs the power track, which is targeted at three separate markets: the commercial building trade, home owners, and industrial applications (e.g. for factories).

The awards are now coming thick and fast. In 1997 the Universal™ Power Track won the $50 000 first prize in the *Yellow Pages* Small Business Award, showcased on Channel Nine's 'Small Business Show'. It is Australia's only high-profile award recognising entrepreneurial and inventive Australians. Then in early 1998 Patricia Strick decided to enter the product in the prestigious Geneva Invention Exhibition. Gledhill Belfanti Productions produced a video and arranged a stand. They went with a contingent of Australian inventors with Beverley Gledhill, Australia's official ambassador to the exhibition. From the beginning it was clear that their product was a popular one. 'Our stand was so swamped that we often had to move people on', says John.

Then came the gala awards night. 'All I remember is Universal Power Track being named the winner of the gold medal award with judges' recommendations. We were still trying to come to grips with that award when we heard our name again! This time for the big one: the Oscar of inventions, the People's Choice. It was like a dream', said John. This was also the first time an Australian company had won the major award.

Along with awards, the business has made some important associations. An Australian extrusion company, able to manufacture large quantities of stock, is now a share-holder.

Asked why he chose to self-manufacture as opposed to licensing his great idea, John says:

> I have found that people like to hold and touch a new product concept. In my experience, this means that you have to have the real thing, not just a sketch, not just a prototype. The real thing. Yes, now that we are operational and we have an actual product, it is very likely that we will arrange very lucrative overseas licensing agreements. But that would have been highly unlikely before.

With all the awards, the shares and the attention, John is now reaping the rewards of a 20-year fight to see his idea become a reality. 'Well, up until recently, everyone in this business was paid more than me. It's nice to finally pull a wage', grins John.

Having proven yourself and your product through self-manufacturing, even on a small level, makes it more possible to tap into government R&D grants and concessional low-interest loans, as well as private investment funds and bank loans.

The initial decision to tool up and do it yourself, versus hitting the road and finding a licensee, will be based on your own resources and lifestyle goals. Like John, you may end up with a mix of self-manufacturing and licensing, so take the time to familiarise yourself with both options.

Invention development and marketing firms

Invention development and marketing firms in general do not have a good reputation among the inventing community. Many people in inventing believe that the large majority are opportunists who take advantage of unsuspecting inventors. However, those that are worth their salt have been instrumental in gaining successful licensing agreements for their clients. Some take a cut from royalty agreements, others work on an hourly rate or for a set fee. Unscrupulous firms require hefty up-front fees, usually for meaningless reports or for making non-existent marketing efforts.

The best way to find a reputable firm is through a referral from an honestly successful inventor, and in particular from an objective source, such as the inventors' associations. The following are some pointers to use when gauging an invention development and marketing firm's bona fides.

- Do not reveal any details of your product idea until someone with authority in the firm (no less than a director) has signed a non-disclosure form, and your intellectual property protection has been applied for or is granted.

- The firm should promptly provide you with professional, easy-to-understand information about its business, which you can consider without pressure or obligation; this material should clearly:
  — explain how the firm works and what it can do for your invention;
  — explain *exactly* how much its services cost (also whether there are any recurring or potentially hidden expenses);
  — give details of the people who will be working with you—their background, years of experience, knowledge, industry networks, qualifications etc.; and
  — refer to past successes that can be verified, such as actual products on the shelves.

- You should be able to visit the premises (granted that some people are freelance workers with powerful industry connections who prefer to come to you, although they should not portray themselves as anything else).

- The firm should be quite willing to provide you with the names, contact details and inventions of successful inventors it has assisted; and you should make contact with as many of these referrals as you can.

- You should not sign *anything* or pay anything without having your solicitor's assessment and advice (warning bells should ring if they tell you that you cannot take a document away for assessment).

- If all is above board and you do proceed with a firm, you should be able to get regular progress updates, understand and be able to query all expenses, and develop a close, working relationship (you should not feel that you are being worked out of the picture).

- Make sure it is clear and agreed to in writing that any improvements made to your invention or product idea while the firm is assisting you become your intellectual property and that you alone have the right to file for intellectual property protection: for example, if a new name is developed and you seek a registered trademark, or a new design is established and you seek a design registration.

InventNET, a handy Internet site for inventors, has a handy fact sheet available on its home page about invention development and marketing scams (www.inventnet.com).

How to find the best possible licensee

If you choose to license your product idea, your goal is to find that one company in the haystack that has the ability and desire to take a risk with you and your product.

Unfortunately, I constantly hear about inventors who were knocked back so many times they lost count. Usually a year or more after they have begun looking, a sympathetic licensee is finally found. But this is just the beginning of the story.

The inventor and the potential licensee must strike up a basic relationship, then move on to the brass tacks of negotiating a licensing agreement. When that is resolved, further R&D will most likely be needed to initiate commercial production. Finally, the licensee must meet the sales targets and all other aspects of the agreement. During any of these stages, the entire house of cards can come tumbling down, leaving the inventor back at the beginning. I advocate pacing yourself and your resources. Recognise that commercialising a great idea is one of the toughest ways to make a living.

To increase your chances of finding a suitable licensee, you should recognise the three categories of licensee:

- those that already make products for the market you are targeting (e.g. a toy company for your game);
- those that manufacture products for themselves or others using the same materials and/or process that your product requires (e.g. injection moulders for a plastic product);
- those that work in completely different areas but have a similar philosophy and/or market, and are willing to diversify (e.g. a greeting card company that takes on a plastic novelty product).

According to Andrew Holt, another form of licensee, slowly becoming more popular, is the consortium. In this scenario, the inventor or a business adviser pulls together a group of individuals whose skills and experience are the key to success. The group might include an accountant, a marketing expert and a manufacturer, for instance. Each makes a financial investment and this forms the basis for some form of payment to the inventor. The consortium then works together to license the invention to another source. This fairly complex concept is appropriate for products that have enormous potential and are well protected. Says Andrew, 'One example of this concept in practice is a product aimed at the surgical industry. This product has been estimated to be worth millions in potential sales due to its significance and the level of the market it is aimed at.'

For many inventors, it makes sense to target a company that carries a similar product line and understands their intended market. As well as identifying these companies through identifying similar products, you may find them on the Internet or while talking with any industry contacts you may have made. In fact, it is through industry networking that you will get the behind-the-scenes information that can make the difference between deciding to contact a business and giving it a wide berth. Andrew Holt has this advice: 'Zero in on the industry. Work out who are the industry leaders and start from the top. I advise approaching three at a time, and then sitting back and getting a feel for how each is reacting.' Once you have identified potential licensees, establish what you know about each, such as:

- how long they have been in business;
- their reputation and recognition among both consumers and the industry;
- how neatly your product would fit into their line-up (and, very importantly, whether your product directly competes with one of their existing products or whether there is a gap in their line-up);
- their market share (as much as you can glean about this);
- their decision-making process, as understood either through your contacts or from telephoning and asking how new product decisions are made.

Because big does not always mean best, be open to the smaller competitors of larger businesses. Often these are more enthusiastic, more flexible, and are actively looking for new products that can give them the edge.

Making contact

If you have inside information on a potential licensee from one of your sources, you will probably also have been given the name of the person to contact. If not, contact the business and ask who handles new product ideas. Then telephone this person and let them know you would like to forward them an information package about your new product idea. Ask what procedures the company follows when evaluating a new product. They may ask to see you and your product idea once they have received your information package, especially if you are in the same city.

During this initial telephone call, ask also whether they are willing to sign a confidentiality agreement. If the answer is yes, send one on immediately through Express Post. If the answer is no, decide whether or not you are willing to take a risk with this particular company. Those who swear by non-disclosure agreements will tell you to walk away now—the risk is too great. Others will tell you to use your discretion.

If a company chooses not to sign non-disclosure forms it may be because it is working on a similar product. Signing your form could make the firm vulnerable to legal action if it proceeds with that idea and you decide to sue. Some firms are just cagey, and others are trying to test your mettle. Regardless, refusing to sign a confidentiality agreement is usually viewed as a bad start.

Once your confidentiality agreement has been returned to you signed and dated, or you have chosen to forgo this, send your information package by registered mail so you have proof that it was received at the other end. Because you have asked what their evaluation procedure is, you will know when to make contact again. But if you feel that too much time is passing without any sign of progress, feel free to telephone your contact. Above all, be professional in your conduct and questions. Don't offer too much ('I'm happy to fly down at a moment's notice'). Never get pushy ('I have to hear from you within a fortnight'), unless you honestly feel you are being given the run around or are being deceived. Don't get too familiar ('How are the kids?'). You also want to avoid sounding desperate. If you have made sound financial decisions by this point, you will have the relaxed attitude needed to view this as a business transaction, not as something on which the rest of your life depends.

The tough nuts to crack

There are some businesses that make it their policy not to accept product ideas except from a small group of coveted inventors and from recognised new-product agents. This is very much the case in the USA, where multinationals like Fisher Price® flatly refuse to have any contact with sole inventors. Access comes only through the small number of toy agents known to them.

One of the benefits of being based in Australia, however, is that the Australian offices of these multinationals are not always so difficult to gain access to. In fact, once contact is made, they may smooth your way with the US head office.

What happens next?

Once you have presented your product idea, either via your presentation package or in person, it will be evaluated intensely by the potential licensee. Expect this to take weeks, if not months.

The potential licensee may be conducting their own

costing analysis to see if it agrees with yours. They may even be conducting initial market research. They will consult their design and marketing teams. They will probably also consult their legal representative to ensure that your product does not pose a threat. And it is highly likely that they have put your idea to their patent attorney and that searches of prior art are being conducted. With your product idea under this kind of scrutiny, it is critical that you have some form of intellectual property protection and the safety of a non-disclosure form.

At some point, your contact will return to you with a positive or negative answer. If the answer is negative, tell your contact that you need your entire package to be sent back to you either by registered mail or via a delivery service, so that it can be tracked should it go missing. However, if they want to move to the next stage, it is time to consider whether or not you want to negotiate on your own, or have a solicitor or other business adviser act for you. Consider this expert advice an investment on your return. It is highly recommended that whomever you bring in is experienced in this kind of negotiation, so ask for a referral from your inventors' association. You are striving for the classic win/win situation, where you get the terms you are looking for and the potential licensee gets what they need to safely take a punt on your product idea.

Get the most out of your licensing agreement

Licensing agreements are formal contracts prepared by a solicitor or patent attorney, and formally bind two parties to a commercial goal. These agreements require specialist expertise, are complex, and must be 'watertight' to avoid later conflict between parties.

Along with referrals from other inventors and inventors'

associations, you may want to contact the national secretariat of the Licensing Executives Society for a recommendation to a member in your area (see Appendix). Members of the society are primarily solicitors and patent attorneys who have specialist skills in licensing agreements. Through this professional association, members are able to continuously improve their knowledge and skills.

The potential licensee will probably ask you to provide the agreement. Having this contract drafted by your solicitor will cost you anywhere between a few hundred dollars and several thousand dollars. Philip Mendes, a solicitor who specialises in technology transfer agreements, advises that inventors should spend their money on solicitors who specialise not just in contract law but in intellectual property:

> Yes, they are harder to find, but their specialist knowledge is worth seeking out. Expect to pay anywhere from $350 and up per hour for a specialist solicitor from one of the larger metropolitan firms. Perhaps a bit less for someone working on their own, or a smaller firm. While it might seem like a punch in the gut to have to pay fees of that nature, remember that their specialist knowledge will make the difference between a contract that gives everyone a warm, fuzzy feeling, and one that inflicts pain if there is no performance, or not the right level of performance.

According to Mendes, a good licensing agreement will also include milestones that the licensee needs to achieve.

The following are some of the features of a successful licensing agreement:

- definitions of parties involved;
- what intellectual property rights apply and are being transferred—patent, trademark, design registration, copyright, plant breeders' rights, circuit layout rights, trade secret etc.;

- length of the licence (usually 18 months to three years);
- territory covered (territory is usually country by country—it is rare to offer worldwide rights);
- non-royalty payments, such as up-front payments, annual payments, non-performance penalty payments;
- royalty rate and royalty payment schedule (usually quarterly, but you may be able to negotiate monthly);
- inventor's rights and responsibilities, including:
  - the right to have the licensor provide you with product liability insurance to cover you in the event of a suit resulting from injury, damage or death caused by your product to a consumer (the protection amount must be in the millions, especially if your product is sold to the USA),
  - the right to be involved and approve refinements,
  - the rights to the final design that goes to market (if your product is refined by your licensee, you will want to own this new intellectual property and any new intellectual property rights that might be granted, i.e. a new design registration or a new patent),
  - the right to inspect and approve final samples before production, and
  - the right to inspect premises and/or audit books;
- manufacturer rights and responsibilities, including
  - high-level product liability insurance (usually $10 million and up),
  - payment and maintenance of intellectual property protection fees or any other regularly occurring fees associated with the invention/innovation,
  - rights other than territory, length of licence etc.,
  - levels of success required (i.e. minimum amounts of units to be sold each year and any related penalty payments),
  - failure to comply (and indemnity issues), and
  - the right to renewal and any other special clauses.

Taking on the risk and excitement of self-manufacturing

The self-manufacturer's action plan

You have now decided to become not just an inventor or product developer but a small business person. The reason why most small businesses fail is because the business operator fails to plan. And almost no small business operators factor intellectual property issues into their planning.

Yes, you need a business plan, but more than that you need an action plan. This plan differs from the main stages of commercialisation (see Chapter 1) because it is solely about starting your business. Refer to Chapter 1 to ensure that you are also on the right path for commercialisation.

The following are some recommendations to help you create your own action plan.

1. Make sure your intellectual property portfolio is up to date; if you have not yet done this, conduct an inventory of your current intellectual property assets and the protection status of each.

2. Make sure your information package detailing the results of your R&D is current and accurate.

3. Write a business plan, either on your own or in consultation with a professional. There are so many helpful business planning guides, books, manuals and software available that you can write it yourself very cheaply.

4. Create a team of experts around you with expertise in accounting, financial, legal, business and intellectual property issues (see the next section for more information).

5. Establish what form of business you want to have—a self-manufacturer with premises, employees etc. or one using direct marketing, the Internet, existing manufacturers, fulfilment houses, telemarketing firms, or

some combination of these. (Make sure you search the registered trademarks database before you apply for any new business or company name. The different databases are not linked.)

6. Establish how much money there is and where the money is coming from.

7. Make a list of all the actions you must take to 'open your doors' to business, when each must occur, and what costs are associated. Tick each off as you complete them.

8. Be on the lookout for new business seminars and attend as many as you can. This will not only educate you but will help you network with advisers you may not have heard about and make contact with other new business operators.

Who can help you start your new enterprise?

Now is the time to seek out the best possible advice from the range of professionals available, such as accountants, business advisers and solicitors. Unfortunately, self-manufacturers have not only business issues but intellectual property issues, and many business advisers in Australia have no experience in this area. Once again, networking and referrals will make the difference between a well-meaning adviser and someone who has the powerful, unique information you need.

For most start-up businesses, finance is essential to ensure that you can pay for good advice and the services you will need later (see Chapter 4 again to review your finance options). A team approach, though it involves a variety of fees, is vital to creating a structure that needs to work from the day you start your business. Later, once your funds are established and you have a direction, you may seek out the services of a graphic designer, marketing and

PR experts, market researcher, and others whose expertise will promote your business and your product to the calibre needed to compete in a tough, lean marketplace.

Low-cost business advice

Business Enterprise Centres (BECs), located throughout the country, are an excellent source of low-cost, often free, general business advice. All run regular, inexpensive seminars about starting a new business and generally have excellent resource material available to buy or on loan. Their networks with other business advisory professionals, such as accountants and solicitors, can be invaluable in helping you to create your team. Some BECs are also connected to business incubators—serviced offices, and sometimes manufacturing space—where a new business operator can start a business with low-cost rent, office support, and business advice on tap. The Canberra BECs are an excellent example of this. Both locations have a mix of office and manufacturing space, where dozens of new business operators have had the opportunity to test the water with their new product or service ideas. Some very successful businesses have resulted from this system and have gone on to open their own premises.

Innovation Advisory Centres, unfortunately available only in New South Wales, are specifically geared to new product developers. They specialise in low-cost technical product assessment, specialised business advice and referrals. They are connected to the BEC network. (See Appendix for more on this unique service and contact details.)

Because some state and territory governments have their own initiatives that come and go, it is best to look in your *Yellow Pages* under small business, business advice, regional development, or simply ring the state government's main helpline.

What federal government money can I expect?

Expect nothing—initially. Other than the New Enterprise Incentive Scheme for people who are unemployed and meet other eligibility criteria, there really is no money available from the government for new product developers. Very often, inventors with the best possible ideas that can involve jobs and a boost to local industry spend hours on the telephone, visit and write repeatedly to bureaucrats, only to find closed minds and closed doors.

Knowing that you are more likely to be successful by just getting on with it will save you a lot of effort and disappointment. After you have developed a strong track record, you will find greater opportunities with government programs.

AusIndustry has a range of programs that can mean subsidised expert advice and cash. (See Appendix for more information about AusIndustry.) Willie Erken and other inventors have received AusIndustry R&D grants worth thousands of dollars. In Willie's case, an R&D grant was granted subject to an objective ergonomic report. This was so favourable that it has had an important positive impact on the product's credibility.

The Department of Industry, Science and Technology (DIST) also has a range of programs. One inventor that I spoke to received a $450 000 concessional loan, which will be enormously helpful to all aspects of his business (see Appendix). Of course, all of this is subject to the government of the day. Keep in touch with the AusIndustry and DIST home pages on the Net, or contact their public relations teams located in Canberra for information packages.

Why small is smart

In the same way that inventors who want to license expect a million-dollar licensing agreement, self-manufacturers should not imagine setting up a major manufacturing outfit with trucks heading out to all parts of the country.

Sue Ismiel is a good example of how you can build your manufacturing capabilities in stages—you couldn't start any smaller than your own kitchen. Later, when she could no longer keep up with word-of-mouth orders, she had her engineer brother make a small version of the much larger machinery she uses in her plant today. Sue then began selling her product at the markets, and later at the malls with her daughters acting as her salesforce. It was only when the time was absolutely right, and she could finance the next stage, that Sue created what would be considered a production plant.

Peter Thorne's award-winning brushcutters are still made and sold on a small scale. He has identified his primary market, and concentrates on steady success in this arena before contemplating moving into other potential markets.

By starting slowly you can refine the product as feedback comes in. This is best achieved by trialling your product in one small market, then tackling larger markets as you build on each success. Even multinationals test products before massive national or international launches. This lessens their risk if the product is somehow not ready for mass distribution, or the marketing is wrong. Australia is considered a terrific trial market because Australians tend to be more sceptical and less likely to impulse-buy. And, within Australia, Canberra is a major test market because of the population's relatively high educational level.

As you start on a small level, you can work out the realities of distribution and learn more about your customers' buying and paying habits. Importantly, you can sort out your advertising and marketing campaigns. Many inventors who are aiming to become self-manufacturers dream of having the money to run a slick, national ad campaign to get the orders flowing. According to Andrew

Holt, instead of a fairytale come true this can spell death to the small manufacturer:

> Imagine if you ran a national ad and were flooded with orders in a concentrated period, say over a couple of weeks. As a small outfit, actually fulfilling these orders could take months. And in the meantime, you are still finding your feet with production, packaging, warehousing, distribution, invoicing and other major issues. The resulting chaos could actually mean customers turn against you as they find that you simply can't deliver.

Slow, steady growth is always viewed more favourably by bank managers and investors. A strong track record doesn't have to be spectacular to be viewed positively by a potential licensee or someone who may want to buy the business. Putting on your training wheels is about being in business for the long haul.

Some of the issues you must consider

The following is an alphabetical listing of some of the issues you may need to confront as a self-manufacturer:

- compliance with all licences, regulations and standards;
- development of relationships with buyers/customers;
- employees, sales and production;
- general bookkeeping, invoicing, accounts payable, debtors;
- insurance (various types);
- legal advice;
- machinery, upkeep and upgrades;
- maintenance of intellectual property protection;
- manufacturing space (or a manufacturing agreement with an existing manufacturer);
- office supplies, including stationery;
- packing and distribution or a fulfilment house that will warehouse, pack and distribute your orders to customers;

- product packaging;
- raw materials;
- service-providers, such as graphic designers, accountants;
- telephone lines;
- wages and tax issues.

A few secrets to reducing your overheads

There are some less traditional ways to establish yourself as a self-manufacturer that can really take the pressure off you.

Max Moorhouse, inventor of protective eyewear, is a self-manufacturer who contracts a local manufacturer to produce, package, pack and distribute his stock. This can be a mutually beneficial association because, along with the products the manufacturer already produces, your product constitutes more work and more stability.

Fairly recently, fulfilment houses have sprung up, mainly to cater to the direct marketing industry. The fulfilment house warehouses your goods, and on receipt of customer orders from you these are processed, packed and sent out to your specifications. Speaking of direct marketing, this is another way to avoid the constraints of traditional business.

Instead of a salesforce with agents and reps and developing relationships with buyers in stores, you direct-market your product to the end-users. This can be done in a number of ways. For instance, with direct-response ads the customer places an order via a telephone number linked to a telemarketing firm or yourself. Through direct mail, the customer places orders through order forms, or again through a telephone contact. Mailing houses have local, regional and national mailing lists for almost every type of consumer you can imagine. Most will even compile, envelope and post your sales material on a per-unit rate. There are also a number of well-known direct-marketing gurus with impressive track records. They use simple, sometimes even old-fashioned approaches to appeal to the consumer.

This form of direct marketing has dramatically increased turnover for some businesses. Direct-marketing firms and freelancers usually charge hourly fees to create your campaign, but some of the more famous individuals may actually require a cut on sales. This is offset by guarantees of major sales. There is a great range of direct-marketing books available on the market and do-it-yourself kits available by mail order from business opportunity magazines. It is a powerful way to create and fulfil sales without the burden of a structured manufacturing outfit.

If you imagine all of these elements working together—your product is manufactured by someone else, the orders come to the telemarketing firm, which sends them on to the fulfilment house to be packed and distributed—you could be lounging on a beach while your product sells like hot cakes. Of course, these services cost, but the cost will generally be significantly lower than manufacturing over-heads and associated costs. Make sure to shop around and get quotes.

Another powerful, non-traditional way of making sales—depending on your product and the nature of your consumer—is via the Internet. A well-constructed home page, one that concentrates on salesmanship as opposed to showcasing someone's artistic talents, can bring in orders literally while you sleep. You receive the orders through your computer and they are fulfilled either by you or through the fulfilment house. You will need to have a credit card facility and be prepared to factor overseas postal costs and insurance into your unit price.

There are several good books sold on the Internet and in bookshops about creating websites that sell. But have a look around on the Net and familiarise yourself with the vast range of websites, from the very sophisticated and expensive to the smaller, one-person-show variety.

Getting a referral to a website designer is highly recommended because, like graphic designers, most are more
concerned with artistic merit than with making a home
page that actually sells product. The last thing you need
after paying your website design bill is a gorgeous home
page and zero orders. Most designers also claim copyright
and will place such a notice on your home page. Negotiate
assignment of copyright beforehand if this is important to
you. And determine how committed you are to using the
original designer if you find you are unhappy with their
services and want to transfer administration and updating
to yourself or someone else.

Appendix

Important contacts: Who's who in intellectual property

The following is an alphabetical roundup of the organisations available to assist you with different areas of commercialising your product idea.

Government and government-funded organisations

IP Australia

This is the federal government body that incorporates the Patents, Trade Marks and Designs Offices. You, or your patent or trademark attorney, will need to make official applications and pay fees for patents and trademark and design registrations.

IP Australia's head office is in Canberra, but there are also state offices in each capital city in which you can lodge applications, ask protection-related questions (but not for advice), conduct free searches, and access some reference materials. To be connected with your state office, ring: 1300 65 1010. Much of IP Australia's information and services can also be accessed via its home page on the Internet: www.ipaustralia.gov.au.

You can ring IP Australia for copies of various do-it-yourself kits for patenting, trademarks and designs. It also has a helpful, free publication called 'Don't give away your most valuable asset', and a helpful, inexpensive CD-ROM which explains the patenting process, called 'Protecting your edge with patents'.

Innovation Advisory Centres

Innovation Advisory Centres were established in New South Wales in 1988 to help people and organisations with new ideas for products or services which they think may be marketable. There are now seven centres throughout the state (see the address listing for the one nearest you). Innovation Advisory Centres provide three main services to innovators and entrepreneurs:

- access to self-assessment software (free);
- business advice and referrals (free);
- low-cost technical assessments (written report $100).

Innovation Services on-line is accessed free via their website: www.ausinvent.com. All information you provide to their business advisers will be treated with the utmost confidentiality.

Ms Jenny Wallace, Manager
Manning-Gloucester Business Enterprise Centre
Tel: (02) 6551 2499
Fax: (02) 6551 2438

Dr Robyn Lindley, Manager
Illawarra Innovation Centre
Business Information Service
Tel: (02) 4227 7413
Fax: (02) 4228 8961

Mr Neil Davidson, Manager
Parramatta Business Enterprise Centre

Tel: (02) 9689 1700
Fax: (02) 9891 3920

Ms Diane Hughes, Executive Assistant
Tamworth & District Business Enterprise Centre
Tel: (02) 6766 2290
Fax: (02) 6766 2262

Mr David Pettett, Business Counselling Manager
Sydney Business Enterprise Centre
Tel: (02) 9281 2111
Fax: (02) 9281 2546

Ms Karen Muddle, Manager
Industry Development Centre (Hunter) Ltd
Tel: (02) 4962 0999
Fax: (02) 4960 1137

Plant Breeders Rights Australia (PBR)

For protection of and exclusive marketing rights to a new
plant variety, you must apply to PBR Australia, a federal
government body within the Department of Primary Industries and Energy. It has a free helpful kit which can be
posted to you.

Plant Breeders Rights Australia
Tel: (02) 6272 4228
Fax: (02) 6272 3650
Home page: www.dpie.gov.au/agfor/pbr/pbr.html

Other organisations

The Australian Copyright Council (ACC)

The Australian Copyright Council is a not-for-profit
organisation which offers free information, training, publications and advice about copyright in Australia. Its services

include free telephone consultations with a solicitor who specialises in copyright issues.
Tel: (02) 9318 1788
Fax: (02) 9698 3536
Home page: www.copyright.org.au

Inventors' Association of Australia

The Inventors' Association of Australia is a national, not-for-profit organisation with state branches. Its main role is to assist individuals and small business operators in getting through the invention and commercialisation process.

It does this by providing regular meetings where inventors can network with other inventors, hear guest speakers who are experts in different fields, gain helpful advice and assessments, and get referrals to industrial designers, manufacturers, prototypers, patent attorneys, sources of finance, business advisers, and marketing and distribution companies. Some state branches have home pages on the Net. Try your local *White Pages* or telephone operator information.

The Licensing Executives Society (LES)

This professional association is a good resource for lawyers and patent attorneys who specialise in licensing agreements.

The Licensing Executives Society
Tel: (02) 9574 9651
E-mail: farmington@compuserve.com

Other helpful sources of information

Government and government-funded organisations

AusIndustry

This is your main port of call for all federal government business assistance programs and services. The AusIndustry hotline uses BizLink, the AusIndustry database. It gives information on all federal, state and territory support programs that are available to assist you with your business. BizLink also gives information on programs offered by industry associations and chambers of commerce around Australia. Contact the hotline on: 13 28 46. The AusIndustry home page is: www.ausindustry.com.au.

Austrade

Austrade is the Australian Trade Commission—the federal government's export and investment facilitation agency, or, according to its mission statement, 'We help Australians win export business and generate inward and outward investment'. Contact Austrade on: 13 28 78. The Austrade home page is: www.austrade.gov.au.

Australian Bureau of Statistics (ABS)

The Australian Bureau of Statistics collects useful data on almost all aspects of Australian life, from population numbers to business sector details. See the government section of your *White Pages*. The ABS home page is: www.statistics.gov.au.

Business Enterprise Centres (BECs)

BECs are dotted around the country. To find the one nearest you, contact your Office of Small Business or your state government's general helpline; check in the government section of your *White Pages*.

Business Licence Centre

This is your contact for all business licences needed to run a business in your state or territory. See the government section of your *White Pages*.

Enterprise Workshop

The Enterprise Workshop is a nationwide program which began several years ago as a wholly government-run initiative, but which is now only partially funded by federal and state governments. Today it is run as a commercial concern by private licensees in each state and territory. Depending on the location, participants pay from $3000 to $4500 to take part in the six-month intensive program. The focus is heavily on business skills.

Through a team format, participants choose a particular product or service idea and learn the practicalities of actually turning that idea into a commercial reality. Their R&D and resulting business plan is of the calibre necessary to seek finance and establish a business.

Ideas and the Investor

This matching service for inventors and investors is run by the School of Marketing of the University of South Australia. For $195, inventors can feature their invention in a pamphlet sent out quarterly to a select mailing list of investors. For a further $20, inventors can be included in the *Ideas and the Investor* home page on the Internet: http://ideas.on.theweb.net. For general enquiries, please telephone: (08) 8302 0712.

New Enterprise Incentive Scheme (NEIS)

NEIS is a federal initiative of the Department of Employment, Education and Training for the long-term unemployed who have a viable new business idea. It involves training and some financial assistance to get started.

Other organisations

Standards Australia

With around 5700 separate Australian Standards, it is likely that your product idea must meet a specific standard before it can be offered to consumers. Stiff penalties apply if your product is commercialised and fails to meet the appropriate standard. Contact Standards Australia for more information: 1300 654 646. Or try the website: www.standards.com.au.

EAN Australia Pty Ltd

This organisation provides barcode numbers for all new products. It is a member of EAN International. National number: 1300 366 033.

Major awards

Yellow Pages *Business Ideas Grants*

Though relatively new, the *Yellow Pages* Business Ideas Grants have proven to be important awards for Australian innovators. Featured annually on Channel Nine's 'Small Business Show', this is perhaps the only national award that has recognised sole inventors. First and second prizes are fairly hefty dollar amounts, providing an important opportunity to bring in much-needed cash to help kickstart your great idea. For more information contact:

Public Affairs
Pacific Access Pty Ltd
Tel: (03) 9246 4888

Geneva International Exhibition of Inventions

This prestigious gathering of inventors from all around the world draws enormous interest worldwide from investors and potential manufacturers and licensees. The event results in awards in several categories. For more information contact Australia's official ambassador to the Exhibition, Beverley Gledhill, on: (02) 9498 2189.

Australian Design Awards

The Australian Design Awards, a division of Standards Australia, is an open competition held annually to reward and encourage the use of professional industrial design in manufactured goods. Judging is undertaken against the following criteria:

- aesthetics and user consideration;
- functionality and design;
- appropriate engineering for economical manufacture;
- value as an example of contemporary Australian industrial design.

Judges are selected from ADA's list of over 150 participating industrial designers. There is a fee for entry. Contact ADA for application details and closing dates.

Australian Design Awards
Standards Australia
PO Box 1055
Strathfield, NSW 2135
Tel: (02) 9746 4991
Fax: (02) 9746 8540
ada@standards.com.au
www.designawards.org.au

State and territory and regional chambers of commerce

Chambers of commerce are an excellent resource for local business networking, training and other services. See your local *White Pages* or *Yellow Pages*.

Top websites for inventors

The following is a mix of Australian and international sites in alphabetical order.

1. **AusIndustry**
   The single entry point for all Australian government business assistance programs and services.
   www.ausindustry.gov.au

2. **Australian Bureau of Statistics**
www.statistics.gov.au

3. **Australian Design Awards**
www.designawards.org.au

4. **Brands and Logos International**
A trademark search and info service.
www.brandsandlogos.com.au

5. **Business angels**
www.businessangels.com.au

6. **Derwent's Patent Explorer™**
www.patentexplorer.com

7. **EAN Australia Pty Ltd**
The organisation that provides barcode numbers for all
new products.
www.ean.com.au

8. **Exciting new products and processes**
www.sgn.com/invent/extra/extra.html

9. **Federal government's business entry point**
Helpful information for business operators.
www.business.gov.au

10. **Help with the American market for inventors outside
the USA**
www.thinkusa.com

11. **IBM Intellectual Property Network**
www.patents.ibm.com

12. *Ideas and the Investor*
http://ideas.on.theweb.net

13. **Innovation services on-line**
Helpful information for Australian inventors.
www.ausinvent.com

14. **Invention Convention®**
www.inventionconvention.com

15. **IP Australia**
The Australian Patents, Trade Marks and Designs Offices.
www.ipaustralia.gov.au

16. **The Internet Invention Store**
www.inventing.com

17. **Invention evaluation form**
www.uspatentlaw.com/evaluation.htm

18. **Inventors' Association of Australia (Qld) Inc.**
www.magna.com.au/~iaaq

19. **InventNET—United States Inventors Network**
www.inventnet.com

20. **Inventor fraud information**
www.inventorfraud.com

21. **Inventure Place**
National Inventors Hall of Fame museum and resource.
www.invent.org

22. **Search over one million Australian businesses**
www.greenpages.com.au

23. **Standards Australia**
www.standards.com.au

24. **State and territory government sites for business information and resources**
www.business.gov.au/government.html

25. **The Small Business Channel™**
www.ideacafe.com

26. **Thomas Register® of American Manufacturers**
www.thomasregister.com

27. **Trade Show Central**
www.tscentral.com

28. United States Patent and Trademark Office (USPTO)
www.uspto.gov

29. USPTO patent searching
http://patents.uspto.gov

30. The Venture Capital Market Place
www.v-capital.com.au

31. Victorian Innovation Centre
www.planet.net.au/~vicidea

32. Wacky Patent of the Month™
'Devoted to recognising selected inventors and their remarkable and unconventional patented inventions.'
http://colitz.com/site/wacky.htm

33. Wal-mart program for first-time inventors
www.wal-mart.com/win/what.html

34. World Intellectual Property Organization (WIPO)
www.wipo.org

Index